BREAKUP POSITIVE

*Turn Your Heartbreak
Into Happiness*

www.mascotbooks.com

Breakup Positive: Turn Your Heartbreak Into Happiness

Cover Photo by Karen Ray Photography

Styled by Allison Rae Marsh

Author Photo by Ben Jorgensen Photography

For more information, please contact:
Mascot Books
620 Herndon Parkway #320
Herndon, VA 20170
info@mascotbooks.com

CPSIA Code: PBANG0118A
Library of Congress Control Number: 2017918471
ISBN-13: 978-1-68401-427-9

Printed in the United States

BREAKUP
POSITIVE

*Turn Your Heartbreak
Into Happiness*

Kris Drewry

"If every twist and turn and bump and bruise and up and down was because I would someday meet you...then the journey, as painful as it was at times, was all worth it."

—J/K

TABLE OF CONTENTS

"Maybe, while you've been kissing frogs and standing in towers waiting to be saved... you didn't see that you have a sword, a horse, and a dream. Maybe it's time to live a story of triumph, instead of a damsel in distress. Maybe, what you seek is yourself, and not a prince.

Maybe he'll show up when you do."

—Mark Groves

INTRODUCTION

"Keep your head up...keep your heart strong."

—Ben Howard

*T*o all of you who are reading these pages with a desire to make a positive change in your life, to turn the pain you are feeling right now into merely a bump in the road that is your story, I write these words for you.

This is a book about transforming your heartbreak into happiness. About finding joy by creating it yourself. About embracing a breakup in a way that allows you to move forward and recreate your life in a positive manner—in a way that lets you take the broken pieces and turn them into something even better and more beautiful than they were before.

My purpose in writing this book is to share the lessons I've learned from my story, to use them to help you get back to happiness. Although the road may get bumpy, you can still find the strength to seek out a new path, because let's just be honest here: *Breakups are fucking hard. Period.*

Whether the relationship lasted a decade or a year or a month, separating yourself from the memories of all those together moments—the lazy Sundays, the errands you would run together, the date nights, the smiles that always came in the morning—is tough. You'll pick up your phone to call them about something only to realize the number you want to dial isn't yours to use anymore. You'll grab at your hand, constantly thinking you forgot to put your wedding ring on that day—a sinking feeling in the pit of your stomach.

It's sad and it's hard, but I want to help you get through it. To show you how you can use a breakup as a positive in your life, a way for you to personally change for the better.

As you read, you'll also begin to see that this is more than just a book about breakups and separating from someone you love or no longer love. It's a book about the happiness that can come from learning how to redirect your steps, grow from your mistakes, and find your footing by refusing to accept negativity or toxicity in *any* relationship, whether it's a long marriage, a short friendship, or a way-too-bumpy new relationship that promises to bring only pain. So, no, this is not just about divorce.

It's a bigger book than that.

I write these words to help you. And if the lessons I share within this book can help even one person feel less alone, less afraid, and more inspired to become their own agent of positive change, then sharing my story will have a purpose.

For me, helping is part of my healing. It's not that I have this huge desire to put such a personal part of my life out there, but if by sharing I can also inspire, then I need to do it because my message is ultimately a happy one.

Don't get me wrong. Bitterness, resentment, anxiety, and depression have *all* played a vital and important role in my recovery and, ultimately, in my long-term growth, but I have no axe to grind. No bitterness here. All of that, as important as it was to feel and to face, has been transformed into something else entirely: a positive story.

And I don't regret one minute of it.

Today, I am whole and happy and firmly anchored in the realization that had I not experienced all that I experienced—the love, the loss, the good, and the not-so-good—I wouldn't be the person I am right now. The friend I am *right now*. The woman I am right now, whose story is a bit different than she expected it to be...but maybe it's even better than I expected?

The fact of the matter is this: I don't see my marriage having failed as much as I see my life *after* marriage having succeeded.

Happy relationships require nurturing, and for those of you who are going through the very real and very raw pain of moving away from an unhappy place, I am here to tell you this: Keep holding on. Keep moving. Keep going day by day. There is a place you can get to that lies beyond the pain, and hopefully the thoughts I share in this book will help get you there.

If you are going through it now, even as you are holding this book in your hands, you already know how quickly the pain can come and how long it can stay...if you let it. You can already feel the shock of its sudden arrival, sometimes at the most unexpected times. Walking down the street on a sunny day and out of nowhere comes the sudden, salty taste of your own tears. Sometimes the pain will leave you gasping for air, for no particular reason—it has a way of sneaking up on you like that.

No, for a long, long time it won't be pretty, but it will eventually transform into something beautiful, if you work at it.

There will be stages. You'll have the highest of highs and the lowest of lows. It might even feel like a death because, in a sense, it *is* a death, it is a loss—and that's okay, too. My message is this: It's all a part of the process. Feel the pain, because the pain is part of the acceptance. Just refuse to stay stuck in it.

Because it does get better. *It gets better.* Not by coincidence or even because of the mere passage of time, but because of *you.* You will change your own circumstance. Take the necessary steps—whether it's therapy or meditation or simply finding a new rhythm that allows you to finally get to happy—that will bring back your balance and, ultimately, your peace.

Obviously, everyone is different. What worked for me might not work for you. But the common bond, the simple theme in all of this is that by pushing through to the other side of sadness and by actually working through it, you will find greater growth and a stronger sense of self.

It won't happen by itself. You must find your own new rhythm. Chart your own new course. Transform that old pain into something bright and beautiful. And eventually, if you work hard at it, you will start to laugh more than you will cry, to look forward more than you look back, to walk with courage rather than with pain. One simple step at a time, one hour at a time, one second at a time until you wake up one morning with a smile and the simple realization that *you will be okay.*

So walk with me now through all of this. Feel energized and empowered by knowing that you can heal yourself. It won't happen overnight, but it will happen if you are active, not passive. Propelled, not paralyzed. Willing to work through the pain, sit in its messiness until you can't stand it anymore, then use it to your advantage.

This much I can tell you from my own personal experience: The darkness will give way to light, and the hurt that happened will hollow out. It will move away. Just don't let it leave before you've taken something powerful and profound from its presence. Don't let it leave you before you've learned the lessons you'll need to live a full and balanced life.

And when it's gone, cherish its departure. Cherish the best part of it and carry it around with you every single day.

xo,

Kris

"And when I looked back at my life, when I looked back at it all, I clearly saw how bad times really meant everything and how every moment that lead me to happiness revolved around some kind of darkness. Sometimes the darkness was a beautiful thing and sometimes it took me to a place where I had no idea where it all could go, but I knew it was all meant to be okay."

— R.M. Drake

CHAPTER ONE

THE PATTERN OF PERFECTION

"Have no fear of perfection. You'll never reach it."

—Salvador Dali

*T*he problem with patterns is they're tricky. If you're not careful, a plain old pattern of behavior can creep up on you and turn into a never-ending bad habit before you've even realized it's happened. That's how sneaky it is. I know this because it happened to me.

When I was a little girl—and I think this only dawned on me fully while I was going through the process of writing this book—I wanted to take care of everyone around me. I needed to be deeply needed. I saw it as my duty, my right, and my responsibility to take care of everyone around me with everything I had—hell, with *more* than I had. I needed to be The Perfect Caregiver. The Perfect Daughter. The Perfect Sister. The One Who Was Always Present.

I somehow felt it was my place in the family, as the oldest of three children, to take care of the people I loved. I couldn't just love my younger brother and sister...I had to mother them, too.

I always had this feeling that everyone needed my opinion on the things that were happening in their lives and needed me to take care of them 24/7. My brother David in particular, seven years younger than me, was not only *the* baby of the family... he was *my* baby. I always thought of him as being my child, not my brother.

For some reason, I got it into my head that he needed me to be his mom, his caring caregiver who was there for him at every turn. The person who picked him up after every stumble. The person who gave her opinion on everything he should do. The person who tried to prevent him from making mistakes. And it almost ruined our relationship. It took me years to fully understand that people have to make their own mistakes and experiences; they have to take care of themselves.

Don't think that my sister was immune to my mothering—she definitely wasn't. However, one of the things I admire most about her is that she (from a very young age) was always independent and didn't care much about what others thought of her. If I'm being honest, she literally did not give a fuck what others thought—she was going to do what she wanted to do and not apologize for it. It's a trait I have always admired and wished I had within myself in my early years. She's one of the strongest people I know because of it. I digress. The point is I could try to mother her, but she just wouldn't have it.

The funny thing is I don't think I was ever frustrated by any of this, at least not as it was happening. I was just *supposed* to take care of everything. It's what needed to happen. It was my role. Simple as that.

Don't misunderstand: I wasn't a clingy child. I wasn't bossy, like many older children are. In fact, I was pretty independent and quiet as a kid, preferring to keep to myself and read books in my room and favoring my stuffed animals over human company. I just always needed to do the right thing and to do the right thing right.

I also felt I had to be responsible for *myself.* I must do my chores on time and do them correctly. Work hard. Get my homework done. Speak quietly. Laugh a certain way. Dress a certain way. Make sure everyone was okay. Worry about everyone and their feelings. And then wake up the next day to do it all over again.

I'm only realizing now just how exhausting that was and how much of an imbalance it brought to just about every one of my relationships moving forward, both platonic and romantic. That's how slippery a path this pattern of perfection can be. Before you know it, it's seeped into your being and traveled with you into adulthood. Taken over. Ruined romances. Broken bonds. Extinguished the possibility of new growth and fresh friendships because now imbalanced relationships are the norm for you.

By the time I'd moved into young adulthood, this pattern of perfection—of needing to be needed—had pretty much settled into my bones. Of course I carried it with me to college. Why *wouldn't* I? Old patterns and bad habits can't be broken until you realize they're old patterns and bad habits and then make the conscious decision to break them up and get rid of them, and that realization just hadn't dawned on me yet. That would take a while (a long, long while) and a lot of reflection.

In college, I was always the responsible one. You could count on me to get you home at night if you were drunk—and since I was in a sorority, this attribute was particularly useful.

Throwing up? I'd hold your hair. Lost your purse? I'd help you find it. Shoulder to cry on? Mine was always there. Sad? Count on me to try to make you smile.

Even after college, as I got a bit older, I was the friend who was always there, coaching you through your problems—the one who'd take care of you when that asshole broke your heart. I'd cook for you. Get you flowers. Sit with you for hours just listening. Wipe your snotty tears away. I'd set aside my needs and plans to take care of you.

The pattern followed me throughout most of my life (like patterns tend to do), and it wasn't just limited to romantic relationships. My driving need to be needed showered (*flooded* might be the better word) just about all of my relationships, romantic and platonic. I *mom'd* my friends to death and actually *mom'd* my first boyfriend in college so much that it became exhausting—for both of us—and we eventually broke up as a result. It was suffocating to all parties involved, exhausting for me, and a burden for everyone. I cared, but I cared too much—I was fully, deeply invested.

The comforting news that comes from these uncomfortable patterns is that, by facing them and breaking them down, I've been able to change them. By pulling them out of the shadows and bringing them back into the light of day, where I get a good look at them and the ravages they caused in so many of my relationships, I can begin to turn things around.

No, I can't change what's already happened or undo the damage that has already been done, but I can learn from the mistakes I've made, and I've been able to take this wisdom with me into the relationships I enjoy today.

Today, I am able to change the depth and direction of my constant caregiver tendencies. Today, I am all about the business of breaking my bad habit of needing to be needed because the trajectory was toxic to me and those around me.

Today, simply being myself is enough for me—whether people like that person or not. Today, I love deeply because I want to love deeply. I don't need to be needed or even need to be loved. I am okay with the person I am, *just as I am.* I am okay just worrying about myself and my feelings—because those are the only things I can actually control.

But this next part is equally important and just as valuable a lesson: Had I not been the little caregiving person I was in my youth, had I not made the mistakes I made and perpetuated the patterns I perpetuated (even though they caused a fair amount of sadness and destruction), I wouldn't be the person I am today—the woman who has learned from her mistakes and missteps and is walking more carefully toward relationships that are balanced and honest.

I no longer have time for toxic trajectories. They took up too much of my energy. But what I do have time for, as I embrace new relationships and find new paths, is the driving desire not to be needed...but just to be *me.*

Yes, I probably still have lots of the quirky traits and habits I had when I was a kid. But guess what? I'm no longer as frightened as I used to be that someone will uncover them as "imperfections." Because they're not imperfections at all. They're more like little mirrors that reflect all the different dimensions of the person I have become, and I'm okay with that. My quirks are a part of my make-up, they are what make me real, what makes me human.

I listed some of these quirks in my blog, *The Fit Butler,* a while back, and they're worth pulling out and dusting off again because every one of them still rings true:

- I have to make the bed every morning, no matter what.

- My horoscope must be read every morning.
  The trustworthy source? *The New York Post*, of course.

- I go into bouts of hysterical laughter for no reason at all
  (typically in public places).

- In my mind, I'm the best dancer on the planet
  (I am actually the worst).

- I am manic about locking doors.

- At the grocery store checkout, I have to arrange things
  in order of how I want them bagged.

- When I get nervous, I say the alphabet backwards.

- I cry for happy reasons, a lot.

- I bounce my knee when sitting because I always have
  too much energy.

- I'm terrible with people's names but have a
  photographic memory.

- I laugh like a lunatic when I get hurt.

- I smile at strangers and talk to everyone.

So if you're feeling unsteady in a relationship or if you're looking for ways to bring balance to an imbalanced situation with a friend or a lover, remember that the pattern of perfection is a dangerous trap. A sneaky bastard. Don't get pulled in. Imperfections are what make you unique and human, they make you...you.

Perfection itself doesn't exist—so why spend (and waste) your life trying to find it? What *does* exist are people who hug too much, friends who need an occasional (but not a constant) shoulder to cry on, and the stranger down the street who needs to see your smile in the midst of their sadness.

What does exist is the simple fact that bringing yourself to any relationship is more than enough and all that you need. Just bring yourself, with all the quirks and imperfections and idiosyncrasies that make up you. Don't waste time searching for perfection because you won't find it, and the exhausting search will just make you sad.

It's taken me a lifetime to learn this (maybe that's why they call them "life lessons"), but I finally see it clearly. It's a lesson that, if it weren't so simple, might be complicated. Here it is, in a nutshell:

"You were born to be real...not perfect."

— Claire Baker

CHAPTER TWO

ALL IN

*"Life is either a daring adventure
or nothing at all."*

—Helen Keller

*W*hen I'm in, I'm all in. Whether it's living or loving or surfing
or even something as little as menu planning for a dinner party
with a few close friends, my habit was to jump in with both
feet—straight into the deepest end of the pool. When I made a
decision to do something, I went after it full force; there was no
stopping me. I worked hard and played harder, with no regret,
no reservation, and very little room (if any at all) for mistakes
or middle ground.

Was it exciting to be like this? Hell, yes. But looking back over
my life and my loves and just about every lasting relationship
or career decision or human encounter I ever had, I realize
this all-or-nothing, go-for-broke approach was also *exhausting*.

Exhausting and not always well-thought-out. I was a make-a-decision-first-then-work-through-the-steps-later kind of girl.

There was a time—not all that long ago, really—when the major events in my life came rushing toward me fast and furious, almost back-to-back, stacking up on top of each other, like pancakes. Again, exciting for sure...but exhausting, too.

At twenty-one, I moved from small-town Virginia to New York City and promptly fell in love with the fast-paced city lifestyle (something I would later find exhausting). I signed a lease before even worrying about finding a job (not the best idea, in hindsight). At twenty-three, I'd met *the* guy; at twenty-four, engaged; and at twenty-five, I was married, starting a brand new career (of blogger/writer and then television contributor) and living the invigorating, sometimes-bumpy-but-always-exciting rollercoaster of a ride that was my life.

Married life was fast-paced and intense. We traveled all the time, to amazing places. Europe was always a go-to. Paris, to see the Eiffel Tower glittering at night. Brussels, where I would eat the most incredible chocolate and pastries. Düsseldorf, to wander the quaint markets during the holidays. Florida, for the Formula One races—always the adrenaline rush. Horseback riding on the beaches of Turks and Caicos. Snorkeling in French Polynesia, helicoptering from island to island. Skiing in Deer Valley during the Sundance Film Festival. We'd go to some of the most beautiful golf courses in the world—some you could only get to by propeller plane—with swaying palm trees, tequila flowing at every hole, and some of the most incredible beaches I've ever laid eyes on.

Sure, sometimes it felt like I was living out of a suitcase, but I preferred a suitcase to a boring set of dresser drawers any day of the week. We played hard, and it felt great...before the balance blew away.

In fact, now that I think about it, I'm not at all that convinced the balance was really ever there in the first place. It wasn't balance I was ever really looking for. To me, moderation was mundane. Why live in the middle of the road when you could race right across it to see if something exciting might be happening on the other side?

Even now, those "extreme" memories remain a part of who I am today, and I don't regret them because they are a vital part of the woman I have become, and there were a lot of them.

Rarely was there a relaxed moment at home, kicking back, watching re-runs. The lazy weekends when I would sleep past 6:30 a.m. never happened—because I was rushing out the door to spin class or getting up to make breakfast. When friends came for dinner, everything had to look perfect. To taste delicious. To feel good and look pretty. Anything other than the most beautiful spread was not acceptable. Casual entertaining? Not an option. I didn't even know what that was.

Not that I ever enjoy playing The Blame Game (especially when I'm the one to blame), but looking back on it, I do realize that the pressures I endured to live such an all-in lifestyle during my marriage were ones I often created myself. I needed to feel needed; I needed to exceed my own expectations and the expectations of those around me. I felt that if I didn't go all in, take care of everything, I'd be shut out. Exhausting, to say the least. Ask for help taking care of things and risk showing I couldn't do it all myself? Not an option.

It was a life of extremes, not only in love but in my daily schedule in general, and over time I began to notice how this all-or-nothing approach touched absolutely every aspect of my life, including my career path.

Hell, in just about every moment of just about every day, no matter what I was doing, I was either all in or not in it at all—no middle ground. Middle ground was boring. I was young, ambitious, adventurous, and completely disinterested in neutral living or slow motion. When it came to living life, why cruise when you could fly?

This—much like the perfection pattern I talked about earlier—began to not only color but *shade* every aspect of my life, from my marriage to my career to how I came to make even the smallest decisions in my daily life.

For a while, the all-in attitude felt like having a healthy buzz 24/7, and I'm convinced I grew as a result. For one thing, it helped to make me feel fearless, not only in love but in life.

For example: When I decided to start working in *front* of the camera (instead of behind it as writer, creator, and photographer), I was giving myself the opportunity to push beyond my comfort zone and to expand into new territory. It was my way of taking a chance and going all in on life itself.

It was terrifying as hell—at first—that decision to put myself out there like that, but as I did it more and more, I began to improve (practice, practice, practice) and gain a more solid footing. Eventually, I became more comfortable on air, and my confidence began to deepen.

But if I hadn't pushed myself beyond my natural comfort level, if I hadn't shot past my own safety zone and stepped in front of the camera (instead of staying behind it), if I hadn't gone all in, said *fuck it* and leaped off that cliff in so many of the crazy ways I did, I'd probably still be teetering on the edge today—that quiet, shy girl from the farm who was always so unsure of herself.

Once I started landing TV shows, I became so excited about booking them that each day felt like more of an adventure than the next. The local shows in New York City were exciting of course—it's one of the largest local markets in the world—but then I started booking national shows—*Access Hollywood, Today, Inside Edition*—and my life opened up even more.

It wasn't a vanity thing. I just got such a high from people wanting to use me on their shows—they liked my ideas!—that it gave me the boost I needed to propel myself forward. It gave me the confidence I needed to keep going after opportunities and do things I never thought possible. Here I was, this small-town girl, and people wanted me on their national TV shows! Dr. Oz cared about my opinions. What?!

It's exactly the same thing with relationships. In life *and* in love, you have to develop the confidence and the swagger that will allow you to take those necessary leaps, make those necessary changes, and create those trajectories that will push you past the places you feel comfortable, even if it means jumping straight off that cliff.

Sure, there's always the chance someone might not be there to catch you when you land—that's not what real relationships are about and not what living a full life is all about—but the important thing is to keep pushing yourself. Eventually, you'll arrive at a new place. Eventually you'll find your footing. Hell, eventually you'll get so tired from all the rushing and excess and overkill that you'll find a way to bring balance back into your life. Sometimes, to get there, you have to go other places *first.*

*

Even my daily life was filled with exciting extremes, from the major to the mundane: As a huge, long-time fan of *Sex and the City*, it wasn't enough for me to just binge watch a couple of shows at a time. No, that would have been too *normal.* Instead—on a whim—I went to a *Sex and the City* movie casting and ended up being hired for the entire day as an extra on the set. Madison Avenue was shut down to shoot for the day, paparazzi were everywhere, and Sarah Jessica Parker told me I had nice legs.

Overkill? Maybe. But it was precisely what I needed at the time, to feel excited and needed, to get attention.

It takes work and it takes time to develop a fearless, fuck-it, I'm-gonna-do-this-thing-my-way approach. It doesn't happen overnight, and it doesn't happen by accident—but once you do it, you'll look back and feel glad that you did.

In a way, when you really think about it, giving it your all is the healthiest way to live your life and one of the most wonderful ways to fall in love—as long as you realize that falling *out* of love might end up being just as important a part of the process.

It's all about the balance.

And as somebody once told me a long time ago (and I saw this sentiment expressed again recently during a random Instagram scroll), *life is a balance of holding on and letting go.* Both are equally important. Both are necessary skills to master if you want to grow. But mastering both requires balance. Do all you can, and at every level of your life, to try to bring that balance.

What lessons have I learned from all of this? How has it helped me in my current relationships? That never asking for help and wanting to do everything for myself was a mistake. It began to feel like an exhausting burden. I was a hamster on a wheel. I felt like it was my job to do everything right, all the time—to serve The Perfect Dinner. To make sure everything was taken care of at home and on the job.

None of this was ever *demanded* of me—I was the primary person who put myself under such ridiculous constraints—and what began to happen was either I was being successful at work and failing at being a Perfect Homemaker and Wife, or I was being the Perfect Homemaker and Wife and failing, in some way, at work. I was chasing a dream, seeking a balance that didn't exist—a dangerous rut to fall into.

In life and in love, dangerous patterns can form. Ruts can be fallen into. Traps and trajectories that are negative and self-destructive can find you, and before you know what's happening, you're flat on your ass, looking up.

There are ways to pull yourself up. Ways to gain enough strength and enough courage to jump off that mountain. Some ways are so simple they will make you laugh. Others are harder. They take a long time and a lot of work. But they can be done.

To bring balance to any life, any relationship, any project, requires patience, confidence, and always, always a healthy dose of humor and humility. It requires that you never, ever feel ashamed by or embarrassed about expecting the most out of life and never hesitating to do whatever is necessary to get it.

Sometimes, in our desire to live a full, all-in life and find that perfectly imperfect romance or relationship, we forget that life itself can feel healthy and happy without being boring. And when we remind ourselves that we should never let success go to our head or let failure go to our heart, living a life of all in intensity becomes a happy challenge rather than an exhausting defeat.

If it should ever get to that, though, if a relationship happens to knock you down, refuse to *stay* down. Finding the middle of the road doesn't mean you have to *stay* there; just use it as a resting place. A place of peace and tranquility.

So when you *do* stumble, or when your all-in life loses its steam or changes its course unexpectedly, let me leave you with these little golden nuggets of humor and wisdom. Turn to them when your life gets out of whack or your relationships have turned raw or angry. Hopefully they will help you as much as they helped me:

KRIS'S QUICK-LIST OF WAYS TO BUST OUT OF YOUR RUT AND LIVE YOUR LIFE ALL IN

1. Fall in love deeply, even if for just a short period of time.

2. Fall out of love in the most spectacular fashion.

3. Make a list of things you want to do that terrify you—skydiving was on mine.

4. Go blonde...or blonder.

5. If you stumble, get your ass back up.

6. Learn a second language.

7. Figure out a new career path.

8. Flirt with the wrong people...and the right ones.

9. Push past your comfort zone.

10. Force yourself past the pain of a broken relationship.

Compile an all-in list for yourself, or feel free to pull from mine. Just remember this: Balance doesn't have to be boring.

"How wild it was...to let it be."

— Cheryl Strayed

CHAPTER THREE

CHASING MARTHA STEWART

"Of all the things I could have been, I am so glad to be this. Thank God I didn't actually become who I pretended to be back when I had no idea of who I was..."

—Rudy Francisco

*W*hat I've come to realize over the years—whether it's been at work or at play, in marriage or in divorce, or standing in this beautifully balanced place I'm in right now—is that you should always remember to be grateful for the stuff that didn't work out. Be thankful for the person you didn't become, for everything that didn't pan out, wouldn't unfold, and couldn't continue, because it's those things that truly create the person you are today. The easy stuff doesn't build character; the hard stuff does.

Dream chasing and goal setting is complicated business. If you're not careful, if you don't keep in close touch with that central part of yourself that should never really change no matter *what* happens in life or in love, you could forget who that person is and what that person stands for. You could lose her. Lose yourself. Lose your footing, your courage, and your core—all before you've even realized what's happened. I know this because I was there for a while, lost in the pursuit of my dreams.

That's the thing with dreams and goals: They're important to have, but you've got to hold on to your center as you're chasing them...or you could lose yourself. In my quest to become who I thought I wanted to become, I almost slipped away from my essential self. I almost didn't remember that person altogether.

Try to be careful.

You can disappear from yourself at any time, in any situation. You can misplace yourself in the middle of a marriage, at the beginning of a new friendship, or while you're trying to just live your life. My point is that a *relationship* (either romantic or platonic) doesn't necessarily need to be involved for any of this to happen.

Losing yourself is an inside job. Finding yourself is, too.

*

Matters of love and matters of life will always, always overlap. They'll always touch each other. Though they're different, they're part of the same whole, completely and totally intertwined. Who you love and how you live are obviously different, but they're also the same, if that makes any sense. They don't exist separately.

This is why the possibility of losing track of yourself is so dangerous. If you're knocked off track in a relationship, chances are you'll veer away from *yourself* a little bit too, at least for a minute. An imbalance in one area usually creates an imbalance in another. How could it not?

The solution, though, is fairly simple: No matter what you face in your daily life, try your best to hold on to your core—even (perhaps *especially*) if you're going through a tough time in a relationship or balancing on a high wire in other parts of your life. Just hold on, because losing yourself is simply not an option. It's only an option if you commit to finding yourself again—and to making positive change in your life moving forward.

As you're reading this, you should make the promise to come back to yourself if you ever veer away. Return to that essential part of yourself that is constant and true and unchanging. It doesn't mean you can't evolve or grow or change. Just the opposite. It means that *as* you grow, you'll commit to holding on to that part of you that makes you *you.*

If all of this weren't so simple, it'd be complicated. I know because I've experienced it firsthand. Otherwise I wouldn't be writing these words. How could I possibly help others if I hadn't been through this in a big way myself?

When I first started in television, one of my dreams was to land a spot on the *Today* show. The producers had turned me down a couple of times. Not in a very gentle way either; they just straight up kept telling me no. But I was more than determined to prove them wrong in their no. Or, to put it more positively, to prove I was the right one for NBC. I needed to prove I could deliver the goods and get the job done. I wanted them to call me back because I *knew* I would work hard, do a good job, and be…well, perfect.

So when the opportunity came up, when I finally heard the yes that would get me on to the *Today* show, I knew a very real dream of mine had been realized.

I'll never forget that first segment. I remember it hitting me, just before I went on air, that an unreachable dream was about to become a reality in a matter of seconds. The opportunity was right in front of me. The goal was about to be gotten. Screw everyone who had ever told me no. I was finally doing it.

If I'm being honest, though, it was more than that. I'd been watching the *Today* show since I was a little girl. It was on our TV at home every morning when I was growing up, an important part of our morning family ritual. This on-air moment would not only be me proving to everyone that I could hustle hard and make it in the TV world, it was proving to myself that I would never let another no stand in my way.

There I was, standing in the studio, my small-town-girl-self ready to step in front of millions of people. (Well, in front of multiple cameras, actually, which would instantaneously bounce my live image to millions of viewers with the simple flick of a switch.) Was I nervous? Hell, yes. *Petrified* might be the better word.

This was the mother of all dreams. The last thing I wanted to do was screw it up. I had placed so much pressure on myself and knew if I didn't do this right, I'd never be asked back on the show again.

But something interesting happened the moment we went live: I swallowed my nervousness. I drop-kicked it away. I decided my dream was bigger than my anxiety and the stakes were too high for any of that I'm-too-nervous-to-do-this-thing-right bullshit. I needed to succeed; I could taste it.

So I transformed all that negative anxiety into positive energy. I made the conscious decision to kick ass and take control of my uneasiness and transform it into something positive that would work for me instead of something negative that would not. Believe me, negative energy and nervousness do not translate well on live TV.

That first segment was about hosting the ultimate fall brunch, and I went all out (of course). I pulled out stops I didn't even know I had. The set was stunning. The tables were set with the best place settings. There was a delicious apple cider bar. Perfectly made pie. It almost looked like a spread straight out of *Southern Living* magazine.

On air, I was chatty and in complete control. I had dressed the part of the ultimate hostess as well. I was having fun. Everything was perfect because I worked my ass off to *make* it perfect. I wasn't about to let my anxiety win. The stakes were just too high for that.

And as I started to do more *Today* show segments (Christmas dessert decorating parties, how to throw the ultimate Super Bowl bash, and other crazy-amazing spreads), something interesting and unintentional happened. This "dream" of mine gradually began to take on a life of its own but with kind of a dark tinge.

It morphed into something else entirely. It got away from me. Or more accurately, I got away from myself...and when that happened, it went from being a dream to being more of a nightmare (a nightmare I didn't even realize I was in until later).

Each segment I did was bigger, better, and more elaborate. I was setting a new standard of excellence, raising the bar to a new level—never mind that largely what I was doing was competing against myself, trying to beat my own personal best (the perfection thing again).

Gradually, as I grew more comfortable and confident on air, I became known for my stylish and elaborate food displays. Imaginative dessert bars. The best home decor. Impeccable presentations. It was all working for me. It was a social media dream, I had the game down—and I was living the life.

Until I began to lose myself.

Without even realizing it at the time, I'd set off on another dream-chasing mission. To be more precise, a Martha-chasing mission. I wanted to be a younger, married, perkier, more *fun* version of Martha Stewart.

I wanted to be the perfect homemaker, to set a flawless table and create the prettiest spaces, both at work and at home. I wanted to make it look effortless. I was going to channel Martha and everything she represented—not so much the person, really, but the *persona*. In my own mind, the banner headline read, "Southern farm girl moves to the big city, meets *the* guy, gets married, becomes the most *chic* homemaker and a television star; she has it all!"

I was already getting away from myself, though the scary part was I didn't even feel it happening at the time. This was simply my new normal.

In television, you always have to be five ideas ahead of your last segment. Everything has to be fresh and fun. I was always chasing the next Perfect Thing, always securing the next Big Goal, constantly prepping for the next Best Segment, without realizing that I was losing the happy, carefree (sometimes messy but okay with it) Kris I once was. I had stopped paying attention to my relationship and was ignoring some of the cracks that were starting to show.

In an effort to find (and redefine) Martha, I was actually losing Kris. I was swallowing myself up whole. I was being perfect but not authentic.

The *real* Kris was stressed out 24/7, waking up at the crack of dawn to begin a day that included working out for no less than an hour, maintaining an impeccable home (or homes really, as we had multiple places), stocking the fridge with groceries, cooking every meal, keeping track of travel plans, staging my segments, and writing producers—always with an eye toward chasing that Martha mantra.

At first, my marriage withstood the rigors. My life was happy and things felt elegant and balanced, but I think that began to wane as I became more distracted and less "with it" at home. As with any marriage, there were other imbalances and challenges beginning to swirl around, but my breakneck speed and stressed-out rhythms helped push me all that closer to the edge, and I simply ignored them.

Even when I felt overloaded and overwhelmed (which was most of the time), one of my biggest mistakes—and, yes, in this rare case, one of my biggest regrets—is that *I never asked for help.* I had told myself I could do it all, and I thought asking for help would sound like an admission of weakness or my being ungrateful for the things that were provided for me by this incredible life of excess that I had.

On the outside, I was kicking ass. Inside, my chest was filled with a ball of stress that just weighed heavily on me at all times—an empty, bottomless hole of pressure. Sometimes I just wanted to run away from it all, or at least escape for a quick minute to get myself back on a normal track, but the train had already left the station, and it was going too fast to stop. (Plus, the perfectionist in me would never have permitted such a slowdown, anyway.)

The faster I ran, the faster I needed to run. I was hungry, tired, and stressed pretty much all the time, and since Martha was my mantra and perfection was my pattern, instead of saying, "I need some help with this," I ended up saying, "Look at me! I'm the perfect wife, the best homemaker, amazing at my job, skinny, pretty, and in complete control of my life!"

Completely in control or completely out of control? At the

time I just didn't recognize it, I was too into myself and this image I was creating.

Big mistake.

So the hamster in my mind made himself at home, running at full speed, and the damned wheel was spinning too fast to jump off. To reduce my velocity so that I wouldn't lose control and cause an accident or an additional imbalance wasn't an option—either at home or at work.

I was focused so heavily on my Martha mantra, on chasing the image of that younger, sassier, stylized persona I hoped to one day become, that I forgot to take my own temperature. I forgot to check in with that person who was trying so hard to become someone else. I lost track of myself.

Where was the self-assured girl who'd packed up everything in the back of her car and moved to New York City by herself? She'd disappeared into this hole inside her own chest. She'd left the building. Slipped away to an undisclosed location from which she might never return. The shit was getting heavy, but I didn't know how to stop it. I didn't know how to stop it because, honestly, I wasn't even aware I needed to. I was leading what I thought was the perfect life and having feelings that I thought were normal.

It was frightening then, but in many ways it's even more eye-opening now when looking back on it and reflecting. Today, right now, I can see with clear vision how much I really had to lose. And what I had to lose was the most important asset I possessed: myself.

And the questions came hurtling toward me in the middle of the night, the ones that had me jumping out of bed at 6:45 a.m. at an insane speed (probably so I wouldn't have to think about them anymore). These terrifying questions had no real answer: *Who is this new person I have become? What the hell am I chasing with such intensity—and why am I chasing it? Where am I running to? What am I trying to prove, and who am I trying to prove it to? Where am I in all of this, again? I know my marriage isn't where it's supposed to be, so why don't I seem to care? What the fuck is happening to me?*

I had an amazing life—of that there was no doubt. But it had become a life without a foundation. I was on national TV, had a successful blog (which started off as *Young Married Chic* and later evolved into *The Chic Wife*), but I'd somehow misplaced my frame of reference. My solid footing had slipped away. I was standing on quicksand, struggling to stand upright. And the dangerous part—the worst part—was that through it all, I was constantly trying to send the signal to *everyone* (including myself, I realize now) that everything was absolutely fine.

God forbid anyone ask me how I was, because *I was fucking fine.* My true friends, girls I had basically grown up with in college, began to slip away because I withdrew from them— they would know I was in fact not fine and could possibly question this life I had built. I didn't want their prying eyes, their questions, because that would mean I would have to be real. I wasn't ready for that, didn't want that.

The strange thing is it didn't really feel like a charade as it was happening. It didn't *feel* like an act because, in my mind, it wasn't—which made the slope I was on even more slippery. This was elusive and deceptive stuff, like a house of mirrors. I was at the top of my game and the bottom of my game at the same time.

Now that I look back on it, I'm amazed I lasted so long. Lasted so long without breaking. It's exhausting to be *perfect* all the time.

What changed? How did I come back to myself? I changed, I suppose. My life changed, and by changed, I mean it blew up in my face. Really, my perspective expanded and time passed, which always brings breathing room and balance. And as all this happened, I gradually adjusted my course, because the life I had known had shattered (heads up, I ended up divorced after all of this).

In fact, a good way to describe it would be a course *correction*—kind of like GPS corrects you after you've made a wrong turn.

*

The process of coming back to myself was not passive or random. It didn't happen overnight. It was driven by my own efforts to save myself, to find myself, to move myself back toward Kris again, rather than the image of a person I was hoping to become.

Today, I am me. Just me. Sure, I'm still chasing dreams, and I'm still evolving, still working hard—I hope I always will—but I'm holding on to that essential part of myself as I'm moving. And as a result, my life is better, fuller. My relationships are healthy and happy. My expectations are high but realistic. And I do what I do for myself, not for others.

Today, I know how to ask for help, whether it's for simple stuff or for major projects. I know how *not* to be a complete and total perfectionist (even in my own head). I know how to openly communicate my needs and not always play the role of caretaker in a relationship. I have learned to be actively grateful for all the dreams I *didn't* find and for all the people I didn't become.

So, here's what I really want to share: In both life and in love, you can never afford to lose yourself. Or let's be a bit more expansive: If you *do* get lost or knocked off center, for whatever reason, use it as a growing experience and make sure you swing back around and return to your essential self while you still can. Make sure you come back to your center.

In any relationship you're in—whether it's toxic or loving or somewhere in between—always remember it's okay to get lost. It's part of the process, really, and an extraordinary way to really grow…as long as *finding* yourself is part of the process, too. It takes patience. But most of all, it takes hard work, perseverance, and a promise to yourself that if you do get yourself lost, you'll find yourself again before too much time passes.

Thank goodness I didn't find the person I thought I wanted to become. If I had, I wouldn't be the person I am today.

"If you don't get lost, there's a chance you may never be found."

— Unknown

CHAPTER FOUR

WHEN IT'S BROKEN

"Everything you want is on the other side of fear."

—Jack Canfield

*C*hances are, if you're reading my words, you've had some experience with the paralyzing pain of a breakup, so what I'm going to say next might sound like I'm singing to the choir. (Albeit, badly. Singing is not one of my strong skills...or a skill of mine at all.)

You probably already know some of the things I'm about to write...but I still need to say it again, not just to get it off of my chest and out of my brain as part of my own cathartic process, but also to put it out there as a reminder to anyone who might be sitting in the middle of their own pain right now:

You are not alone. You will get through this. There is a place on the other side of all this and, eventually, you will get there.

It will be hard and there will be many stages, but you will get there because, quite honestly, you have to in order to heal. You are in control. You are not a victim.

Changing course in a relationship—any relationship—hurts like hell; it's one of the loneliest life experiences you'll ever encounter. Whether the relationship was good or bad, healthy or unhealthy, in need of a little work or ridiculously, irreparably damaged, coming to the end of it is awful.

It doesn't matter who was at fault or who fucked up or who left whom. Sure, those things played a role in the split, but if you've found yourself at the end of the road (a very scary place to be, at least at the beginning), none of those other factors really matter anymore anyway.

Coming to the end, for me, created haunting questions that shook me to my very core: How could I fathom a future being single after being with the same person for the last nine years of my life? What did flying solo even *feel like?* Even if it wasn't perfect, it was my *life*. It was all that I knew.

I was also in that stage of life when everyone around me was either married, getting ready to be married, or having kids. Everyone was fluffing their nest in one way or another, either by creating a new nest to make space for kids or sprucing up the one they had so they could settle into married life. And now suddenly, my nest, my space, my solid union had come undone. How the hell had this become my new reality?

Of course, to be completely honest, I had chosen this new path. It didn't just happen to me. But sometimes it felt like it wasn't a choice really, just something I had to do in order to not suffocate, something I had to do to save myself—to save this person I'd put on the back burner for such a long time. It is terrifying to have to make a decision like that, and I think the one who leaves or makes the decision to end it will always be left with a lot of guilt. It's something I still live with.

Being in a romantic relationship was a pattern that had always felt familiar and comfortable to me, even if the relationship itself had grown uncomfortable and unfamiliar. For me, being alone wasn't really ever a consideration...or at least not an attractive alternative. It wasn't a rhythm I was used to. Being in a relationship always helped define me because I'm not sure I ever really knew who I was exactly, and I never really took the time to get to know that girl.

Even in my college days, I felt off-balance if I wasn't attached to someone else, which is kind of crazy when I think back on it because I never had boyfriends in high school. (With thirteen kids in your graduating class, who was there to date?)

After my first college boyfriend and I broke up, I realized I felt incomplete if I wasn't a girlfriend, a caretaker. If I wasn't standing at someone else's side, where was my space in the world, my purpose? This question followed me—haunted me—as I moved to New York City to start a new life and a new career. Being single in those early days was so lonely for me.

If I wasn't a wife, who was I? That question would come at me daily after the split, sometimes hourly, as I grabbed my left hand thinking I had lost my wedding band. Who...was...I?

For one single reason, or a million reasons, I never allowed myself time to heal between relationships. I never gave myself the luxury of taking the time to discover who I truly was without another person at my side. I needed to be constantly, firmly attached, like a barnacle on the hull of a ship.

And here's an interesting distinction you might be able to relate to: It wasn't necessarily the prospect of being alone that scared me when my marriage ended. (I've always been a pretty independent person, and I actually spent a lot of time alone, even when I was married.) It was more the shock, the sadness, and the anger at having arrived at the very end of that time in my life.

All of a sudden, it was my reality. I was only thirty-two at the time, and when the end of marriage became real, when we finally reached the end of *our* road, I was sure that I'd also reached the end of *my* road, too. I thought my chances of being a partner, a wife, and someone's constant companion were over forever. I thought I was destined to fly solo. I couldn't even fathom being with another person at that point.

During the actual split, there were days when I felt like a huge weight had been lifted off my shoulders and out of my heart. It was almost a sensation of being unburdened of a heavy load, a feeling of lightness.

But there were other days I could barely move. I could barely breathe. I could hardly think. I felt like I'd experienced death—either the death of a loved one or my own death, really—because that's what the end of a relationship is.

It is a death, and don't let anyone tell you otherwise.

Some of my darkest days were just after the split. During much of this time, I kind of shut down. I couldn't eat. I was drinking a little too much (and as someone who never drank, anything was kind of a bit too much). I remember it was even difficult to cook for myself, which was really unsettling because I've always loved cooking. It took months for me to enjoy even going out to buy the ingredients for a meal—something I used to love to do. I wanted nothing to do with anything that would remind me of my old life.

I was terrified, sad, scared. And angry. I was so angry. I'm not even sure who was I angry *with*—it almost didn't matter—but I was fucking mad.

I had days I couldn't see straight because I was in so much pain. And here's a message I need to share with you about the shitty part of breaking up: Every one of these awful emotions was important to experience. Were they almost unbearable? Yes. Did they feel like they'd never end? Yes to that, too. Did I feel like I was dying sometimes? Yep. It seemed like a never-ending cycle of pain.

But eventually the feelings *do* end. The anger and the fear and the sadness transform into something else. And although each one of us will experience the progression at different times and in different ways, what I can tell you is this: Slowly but surely, you'll return to something that feels right and balanced—your new normal. It won't be your old normal, but it will come. And it will work.

It will work, but it doesn't happen on its own. You've got to *make* it work. Push it forward. Create your own positive momentum.

Here's the other thing: If you're going through what I went through, if any of this sounds familiar in your own life, you need to know that *sitting* in this stuff, staying in the middle of this messiness for just a while, is an important part of the process.

Don't try to bottle it up or avoid it because that is just denial and it will come back to bite you in the ass later. Don't feel guilty or embarrassed by the intensity of it all. Just know that those dark moments are *okay*.

I'm grateful for the fact that I faced my fears and was able to sit still, at least for a little while, in the midst of all that darkness. I just had to make sure I didn't let too many of those days stack up on me. For this very reason, it was important for me to at least try to stick to some kind of normal routine, even if I had to force it.

I'd work out. Meet a friend for lunch. I'd hit up my favorite coffee shop, even if I didn't need a coffee. I needed to get outside of my head and my heart and all the pain that was swirling around me, if only for a minute, because it all would sure as hell be there waiting for me when I got back.

So there was a balance there that was vital for me to achieve in the midst of such dramatic imbalance—even if that balance was fleeting. Again, it didn't come automatically or even organically. I forced myself to find those moments. I forced myself to find the escape hatch and create a mechanism to push through. You can do it, too. *This* is what will help carry you over to the other side of your pain. It'll be the tiny steps that will get you over the bigger moments of darkness.

For me, reaching out to others was important. Instructing kids at surf camp—something I took up during the summer— gave me something productive to do (plus, it's almost impossible to be sad when you're around kids). Teaching surfing was therapeutic for me, and I'd like to think that it brought the kids some joy, too. To this day, being in the ocean is still my happy place.

Babysitting or meeting a friend for coffee (not for an advice session, but just for the simple act of being in another person's company), for example, were small but important ways for me to decompress and refocus.

I had to have them.

*

My other message is this: Your pain can be empowering.

If you come at it with the right attitude, if you come at it with the recognition that the pain and the anger and every other emotion in between is necessary and justified, you'll remain strong enough to *not* let it define you. Instead, you can let it work for you.

So feel it. Absorb it. Even let it kick your ass for a minute or two, but refuse to stay stuck in it. And then, when it's finally worn out its welcome, send it packing. Send it somewhere else, to another place. Remember that you have the ultimate control. If you're facing the prospect of your own sadness, know there is a bright side to all of this darkness. At some point along the way, something shifts. Something *drastically* shifts.

After the anger subsides and the smoke clears, what will eventually arrive—if you invite it, create it, and keep your eyes open for it—is a feeling of empowerment.

The realization that we can't really ever control other people, that we can't control how life will evolve or unfold or present itself shouldn't be frightening—because we still hold the trump card. We still have complete control over how we *react* to these life changes and how we respond to unexpected adversity. What could be more empowering than that?

It is this element of control that will help get you through. No one else will do it for you. It will be yours to own. You can choose to spend your days in bed—I certainly had many of those days—but you can also, eventually, choose happiness, too.

I urge you: Choose happiness.

*

I remember someone saying something to me on a particularly bad day. It was my wedding anniversary—the first one since the split. I'd just met this person, but I still carry their words with me to this very day:

"The good news is that this isn't the end of your story."

In other words, no matter how bad things were or how bad they were going to become, my story was not finished. Even today, I'm still a work in progress. My story isn't over. In fact, it's just really beginning.

Always remember that, especially when the dark days come:

You're always in charge of your own story.

"True power is living the realization that you are your own healer, hero, and leader."

— ***Young Pueblo***

CHAPTER FIVE

THE FUCK-IT PHASE

"If you're going to rebel, do it with purpose."

—*Unknown*

ME: *Heyyy! I'm in the city and going to stop at that new vegan dessert place on MacDougal Street...I'll get us some treats before I head back out to the Hamptons.*

(About fifteen minutes later.)

ME: *So I got a few different cupcakes and cookies...oh, and I got a little something at the tattoo place next door to the bakery, see you in a bit!*

(Sends photo of wrist being tattooed.)

ASHLEY: *Wait, I thought you were just getting dessert?*

Yep, I got the tattoo.

That "VII" tattooed on my wrist was now stamped there for life. Maybe I got it in an impulsive moment, but I placed it there so I could look at it and say to myself, "It's all good," on a daily basis (as a 7/7 baby, seven has always been my lucky number). I had no one around to tell me *not* to get it, so I thought, *Fuck it. Why not?*

On my way to the Hamptons to hang with my friend Ashley (who was crucial to what I call my rebellious "tattoos-and-tequila" phase and my closest friend during that difficult time), I went for treats one evening and came out with, well, a tattoo. On MacDougal Street in NYC there happens to be a plethora of college kids, tattoo parlors, and, randomly enough, a vegan dessert spot. One-stop shopping—for me, anyway. Who knew?

It was an intense period. By the time I was done with my relationship, I was really, really done. I just remember feeling so fucking *angry* during this time—angry at one thing, at a million things, at nothing in particular—that I wasn't even thinking straight. And I didn't *want* to think straight. I needed my thoughts, my words, and my actions to feel a little crooked and off-balance. I needed them to feel out of line. Over the top. Upside down, even. Anger can be a powerful thing, as it propels you out of sadness, and it can actually be very useful, if you don't stay in it for too long.

Sometimes, a good friend can save you from the worst parts of yourself. In my case, my friend Ashley helped me tap into a part of myself I really needed to access at that crucial time.

The *rebel* Kris I called *Kiki*. (Kiki is an old nickname and still kind of like my alter ego, which I love.) Rather than the traditionally quiet, easy-going, okay-and-under-control Kris, Kiki didn't give a shit what anyone else thought. She was free, fun, a little wild. Still is.

Ashley was my favorite counterpart during this fuck-it phase. She was (and still is) my go-to whenever I need a laugh. She's a straight, no-bullshit sharpshooter and one of the smartest people I know. To this day, I'm not even sure she realizes how much she did for me during this time in my life. She was there by my side and simply let me be me, without asking too many questions. Without trying to be my therapist. Without trying to fix or solve or address or analyze any of the shit I was going through at the time. That, to me, is the role a true friend should play. All the time.

She gave me total freedom to be myself. She gave no apologies and did not gloss over anything with "you're going to be okay" platitudes. She just let me be, and she helped me have fun while doing it.

The beauty of writing a book like this, for me anyway, is not only sharing my story in a way that will offer strength and hope to others as they make their journey, but to acknowledge and embrace all the good that people gave me when things were really, really bad—people like Ashley, who helped keep me afloat and who stood with me as I tried to absorb all my anger without trying to lead me to some new "healing place."

During this white-hot time, I could have been in hell. Instead, I found myself in the Hamptons and hanging with Ashley who helped push me through the pain. Even today, I remember our time together with love, with laughter, and with relief (thanks, Ash).

I call it my "Fuck-It Summer."

They're not just memories, though. They're a very real part of how I healed, and they created a sense of stability and strength that remain with me today.

I remember playing in the ocean, laughing our asses off as we tried to balance on the same paddle board while doing yoga;

eating donuts at the 7-Eleven at 2:00 a.m.; ordering hamburgers with bottles of wine at our favorite restaurant on a weeknight because, well, why not; dance parties in the kitchen with the music blasting; busting our asses at our favorite workouts while wearing crazy-printed Spandex; playing, laughing, and (me) crying; eating pizza; and scream-singing to *Pursuit of Happiness* by Kid Cudi while driving with all the windows open in her Bronco:

Living my life, getting out dreams
People told me slow my roll, I'm screaming out "Fuck that"
I'mma do just what I want, looking ahead, no turning back
If I fall, if I die, know I lived it to the fullest
If I fall, if I die, know I lived and missed some bullets

I'm on the pursuit of happiness, and I know
Everything that shine ain't always gonna be gold
Hey, I'll be fine once I get it
I'll be good
I'm on the pursuit of happiness and I know
Everything that shine ain't always gonna be gold
Hey, I'll be fine once I get it
I'll be good

*

It was an intense period; that's the best way to describe it. I might as well have had a big "fuck you" written across my forehead in Sharpie: Fuck you to my old life, fuck you to my ex, fuck you to all of our mutual friends. Fuck you to taking care of anyone but myself.

I felt like I'd taken care of everyone else for years—my husband, my family, my friends. I wanted (and needed) to be selfish. I needed to worry about only one person, only one thing:

My fucking self.

I wanted to work out, surf, drink tequila, eat tacos in the sand barefoot, flirt with people...then wake up and do it all again the next day. I was fucking done with being so fucking good.

I realize now that this attitude wasn't the best or the most respectful way to deal with things, but that hot ball of fiery anger just sat in my chest, and it was the only way I knew how to deal with it at the time. Maybe it was the only way I *should* have dealt with it.

Instead of looking back on that time with regret, I look back on it as more of a necessary phase...though, with apologies to whomever I might have hurt. Sure, during that time I did some things I'm not particularly proud of—drank a little too much, caused a little too much hell, kicked up a little too much dust (or in my case, sand), but I see *all* of it as part of my learning experience and my story, so who am I to say that it was so wrong?

My furious "Fuck-It Phase" was even a subject in my blog. Here's an excerpt:

When I looked at my life, I felt like it was just passing me by, like was just "happening" to me. So, I decided to live by a new mentality for a while, one that is not very eloquent but worked for me on my darkest of days.

Fuck it.

You read that right...fuck...it.

Dessert in the middle of the day—fuck it, delicious. Skipping a workout to lay on the beach—fuck it, yeah. Going out on a Tuesday night for tequila—fuck it, absolutely. New tattoo? Fuck yes. (Sorry, Mom.) Learning something new that terrifies me like how to surf—fuuuuuck yeah (screaming, laughing as I fall off my board time and time again).

So yeah, it's safe to say that this new motto can get scary at times—as it's basically saying yes to all kind of things I never would have before. However, staying in your comfort zone doesn't create change. Guess what does cause change? Being fucking scared.

Life throws things at you that you might not ever be truly ready for, keeping you on your toes. It forces you to make decisions that you aren't ready for—but if you are just going through the motions of every day, the same motions over and over just to stay safe...is that really a life?

*

The funny thing here, the ironic thing, is that this was not my first fuck-it stage. Oh, no. This was a cyclical thing; I'd felt this momentum before, when I was in college.

By the time I left for college, I think I was so sick of keeping it all together, of always being the "good girl" and following all the rules, that I was more than ready to explode into Bad Girl Kris.

I was ready to become Kiki.

So, I dyed my hair blonde. Got a tattoo. Pierced my belly button. Started drinking a little too much. I did just about everything then that I did post-divorce. The pattern persisted.

Truth be told, I am still kind of a rebel today. I'm sarcastic, straight-shooting, and I don't need to be a people-pleaser anymore. I speak my mind. Stand up for myself. Refuse to deal with bullshit and hang-ups anymore. I won't be disrespected by anyone—and I'll always tell you how I'm feeling, even if my feelings might not be right or well-received.

What I did back then helped me get to where I am today. All

the anger and pain I experienced transformed into something more lasting and substantial—which proves that this period was necessary. It was constructive, not destructive.

I needed to be Kiki then.

She was fun, but she was kind of a selfish asshole, too. Whatever the case, she was precisely what I needed at that time in my life—both times in my life—and I wouldn't be the person I am today if I hadn't been that person I was yesterday. I wouldn't be the Kris I am today unless I'd been the Kiki, too.

The lesson in all of this? That anger is important. It is necessary. It's just not productive to *stay* there because it means you aren't healing. So if you *are* mad, then *be* mad! Own it. Have some fun while you're at it and then continue the journey back to being okay.

If I could do it all over again, I'd keep the badass, fun aspect of Kiki, but I'd probably tone down some of the decisions she made. Everyone and their mother didn't need to hear about every little detail I was going through at the time. They didn't need the unflattering mentions of my ex or some of the unnecessary excess. *That* badass probably should have expressed herself a little differently, a little more constructively.

So, if you do go through this phase, try to pay attention to who you might be hurting with your actions because it's really not *just* about you. Your actions affect other people, too. Maybe this is something you don't care about at the time—I know I didn't—but I wish I had. I wish I had someone whisper to me during my fuck-it phase, *"Be where you are in your pain and your anger. Just don't let your behavior cause pain and anger to others as you express it."*

This is my reason for writing this book—to share the life lessons I know now but didn't know then. To encourage you to embrace every single phase in the cycle of your own breakup in a way that is constructive but not caustic, authentic and real but not cruel to others.

Like I've said before, it's all a part of the process, part of the organic cycle of a breakup. Everyone's cycle is different, but in a way, every cycle is also universal.

So embrace your fuck-it phase if you happen to encounter it. Get lost in it. Surrender yourself to it. But come out on the other side, and always, always be aware of who you might be hurting.

Let your anger work for you, not against you. Know when to walk away from it.

In short, be a badass without being an asshole.

"I must also have a dark side if I am to be whole."

— C.G. Jung

CHAPTER SIX

WHEN PRIVATE BUSINESS BECOMES PUBLIC

"Trust yourself. You know more than you think you do."

—Benjamin Spock

*B*reaking up is (or should be) a private affair. The pain is yours alone, and so is the fear, the shock, and the sadness that comes along with it. Eventually, though, *other eyes* must see it. Other ears must hear about it. Other people must absorb the news and process this news however they see fit—even if you don't want them to.

Whether it's a family member, a good girlfriend, or a complete stranger with a way-too-passionate plan for how (or if) your relationship should end, everyone's going to have an opinion about what could have been salvaged or what should have been saved. Everyone will have a question about how in the *hell* such a match made in Heaven could have come so completely undone, gone so wildly off track, and become so unhinged in the first place.

Resist the urge to get pulled into the debate. Resist the urge to answer to anyone but yourself. Learn to listen to—and trust—your own inner voice rather than the noisy voices of those around you, even if they're well-intentioned (well-intentioned but so fucking annoying).

I need to say it again: Learn to listen to yourself. Turn away from the pull of the prying eyes and opinions of others. Trust that quiet voice within, even if that inner voice has been reduced to a whisper (or a whimper), teach yourself to listen for it anyway because it is all you have and all you need. Learn to listen to yourself. This will help get you through. I know this because it is precisely what helped pull me through the worst of it all.

It took me a long time to realize I could not control how other people reacted to the news of my divorce and even longer to realize (and appreciate) that even if I could have controlled them, I wouldn't have wanted to anyway—it would have used up too much of my energy on something that didn't matter at the end of the day.

All I can control is myself (and worrying is just a false sense of control). The only place I need to be is precisely where I am at this moment, in this space that is my daily life. All I want to do is live a balanced life with courage and grace, a life of meaning and purpose that is defined not by what others think about me but by how I relate to myself and to those in the world around me.

If you are in the middle of a breakup, or if the private matter of your breakup is about to become public, all you can do is manage your own affairs and listen to your own voice. The other eyes will look anyway, and they will see what they want to see. The other mouths will form sentences and offer advice and share words of wisdom that are (usually) meant to soothe and protect you during this awful time. But resist the urge to fall prey to their wisdom. Or at least learn to listen to your own voice *first*.

I know the potential problems with receiving advice and "wisdom" because so much of it came showering down on me during and immediately after my breakup. And as much as I appreciated the effort, as much as I wanted to embrace and accept these gestures of love and wisdom, I'm now so very relieved and grateful that I didn't because no matter how well-meaning the words or how sage the advice, it wouldn't have been applicable to my own unique experience anyway. I needed to make decisions and come to conclusions myself, not because someone else told me what those decisions and conclusions should be.

The square-peg advice of my friends and family just wouldn't have fit into the round-hole reality of my own experience because the simple fact is, as human beings, *we are all different*. We each come to a relationship—whether it's the beginning, the middle, or the end of a relationship—from a unique place with a unique set of circumstances. Your place of understanding is not mine. Your frame of reference does not belong to me. They are not interchangeable.

For this reason, the shape of your solution will not always fit the shape of my problem. Nor should we really expect it to. What works for one person doesn't always work for another. One size does not fit all when it comes to solutions.

The challenge with female friendships is that we too often tend to create a tribe mentality, which actually ends up doing more harm than good because it prevents us from making decisions of (and on) our own.

Although it may be an unpopular belief to have, I'm just going to go ahead and say it: During both good times and bad, many women have a really bad habit of relying on their girlfriends for value and validation. This only creates the expectation that they need to ask permission from others to proceed.

The trouble with tribes is they instinctively rely on each other for protection and guidance, and they forget that giving someone protection and guidance is very, very different than giving someone the *truth*.

Even if your tribe comes to a proposed solution for your problem from a place of love, even if all they want to do is make you feel better about your breakup and heal your hurting heart at any cost, their protective instinct shields you from what you need at that very moment: the raw truth, open space, and a clear head so that you can plot your next steps or simply just sit in your own pain.

Were my relationships with my girlfriends important during my breakup? Of course they were. But not for advice-giving. Not for guidance. When I was going through my divorce, I relied on my girlfriends as a happy (and, yes, necessary) distraction. I needed them to be there for me. I needed to know they were there for quality time away from the bad stuff, to let me laugh or cry or just *be*, for no reason at all. I needed to vent to them, occasionally, but not to solicit or receive their advice.

The advice (or guidance really) that I needed, I got from my therapist. A non-biased person who would make me come to conclusions and decisions on my own by asking me the right questions and forcing me to sit back and think.

People who really care about you, who really want you to be happy, do not *want* to see you sad! Their instinct is to pull you from the brink of sadness and depression immediately, rather than to push you over the ledge or even let you linger for a minute at that uncomfortable point.

Sometimes, though, it is healthy and necessary (though not always comfortable) to *be at that brink*—and even to tumble into the abyss. Sometimes the sadness and confusion are the necessary byproducts of a breakup; they are obstacles that actually *belong* in the middle of the road. The challenge is to figure out a way, on your own, to get through the obstacles. To get around them. Walk by them. Kick them the hell out of the way on your own, rather than relying on your girlfriends to do it for you.

What I'm saying now is what I've said before: To get through the pain, sometimes you have to sit right at its raw and ugly center in order to push through it and eventually arrive on its opposite side. This, in my mind, is the only authentic way to walk toward healing and health. A tribe will not—*cannot*—do that for you.

What I didn't need at the time of my breakup was to be given advice that would just make me feel better. My wounds were deep and the pain was real. Putting a little Band-Aid on pain like mine wouldn't have healed my wound; it would have made things worse. At the time, I didn't need to be *better.* I just needed to *be.* I had to give myself permission to not be okay.

I do believe that it helps to talk it out with someone, but I don't always agree that your girlfriends can give you the best advice either. Their judgment is clouded by their love for you, their need to protect you, and by the depth and breadth of their own unique experiences and encounters, which are simply not yours.

Sure, I would cry and vent and be real with them, but I would also say things like, "Although I appreciate your advice right now and as much as I cherish our friendship, this is something I need to work through myself."

I remember having a very opinionated friend during the time of my breakup, who I don't have much communication with today. Every time I made a decision (or didn't make one) she would offer up aggressive, unsolicited advice. I finally had to say to her, "Although I appreciate your opinion, please understand that I am not *asking* for it, and I would really like to figure this out on my own."

It was a way of shutting her down (and shutting her up) without being too mean or caustic or cruel. And I owed it to myself to be completely honest with her. This is why it's so important to be direct and unapologetic with anyone and everyone around you who tries to step in close with well-meaning advice during this challenging stage. You're vulnerable already. Don't make yourself more vulnerable by seeking permission to proceed.

On this topic, on the task of dealing with the advice-givers, I urge you to be clear and concise in your communication without being cruel. Try saying something like this: "Unless I'm asking you for your opinion, please try not to give one. Please just sit here with me and be my friend."

During tough times, people tend to underestimate the power of the little stuff. They tend to forget what a big difference a small gesture can make.

I remember a girlfriend of mine really going through a rough patch. Instead of offering her my opinion and my super-sage advice (not), I'd do little things that hopefully made a big difference.

Some nights I'd have dinner cooked when she got home from work. Or I'd buy silly coloring books and we'd spend the evening eating salads and coloring. We'd meet for an exercise class or a glass of wine after work. It was my way of showing that I cared—deeply—without exhausting her or burdening her with my opinions. I'd only give them if she asked for them. Otherwise, I was just there for her. When I was going through my breakup, this was the kind of stuff I needed. I tried to keep that in mind when dealing with friends in similar situations. Sometimes just having a friend sit with me and *be* with me was all I really needed from them. Just their simple presence; nothing more, nothing less.

*

When your breakup moves from a private matter to a public issue—even if it's just having to finally share the news with friends and family members—the chemistry of the breakup itself begins to change. There is a shift in its energy. It is no longer organic. People will feel the need to weigh in, to redirect, to shift the focus away from the thing that is and focus instead on the thing they want it to become. They'll want to save you from yourself.

It's easy to get caught up in asking everyone and their mother for their opinion—but as I mentioned earlier, this is not the best option. And here I need my language to be plain and simple yet again: *Stop asking for permission.* You do not need others to make decisions for you. If you don't trust yourself during something as tough as a breakup, you never will trust yourself at all.

Not trusting yourself could possibly be why you're in this spot in the first place. Remember, what happens now, what happens at this critical juncture when a breakup becomes a matter of public scrutiny, is a true *test of self.* You will only be able to live with and accept your decisions if you are making them by yourself. You're an adult, a grown-ass human being. *Own it.*

Therapy is another thing that helped pull me through. Although I know it's not an option for everyone—maybe your insurance won't cover it, maybe you're having problems finding a good one you really trust, or maybe you're simply not yet comfortable with the process—but during the Summer of the Split, as I call it, therapy (and surfing, but more about that in the next chapter) is what saved my life.

My therapist's opinion is the only opinion I sought aggressively and consistently throughout the entire breakup. She did not bullshit me and would call me out when I was wrong. At the same time, though, she let me make mistakes, fall on my face, and pick myself back up. She was a priceless resource for me, and someone who will always have a place in my life, even (perhaps especially) when things are good.

I truly believe that I would not have made it out of the Summer of the Split if it weren't for her empowering me to *believe in myself.* To not apologize for my decisions. To tell me that it was okay to finally be honest with myself and with others. To give myself permission to rely on me.

To this day, I still have a standing monthly check-in with her, proof positive that her trained and balanced approach not only helped me then but is still helping me now. I need her today as much as I needed her yesterday. That knowledge, in and of itself, is a gift. It is a gift that makes me stronger, not weaker. It is a gift that makes me more independent, not dependent. It empowers me and sharpens my vision.

If you're stuck in the middle of the quicksand and fighting like hell to break free, if you're surrounded by well-meaning advice-givers, solution-seekers and fiercely protective members of your own, loving tribe, let me also gently suggest that you at least *consider* expanding your circle to include a good therapist, too.

And if you find one, hang on to them. Do not just talk to them when things are bad. Make their professional opinion a part of your regular rhythm. Tribes might be good in times of trouble, but their function should be specific and well-defined. Therapy is one thing. Tribal protection is another. Both can work, just not at the expense of each other.

*

I need to share something else while we're on the topic of mental health that is a part of my own truth and my own past that eventually really *did* set me free: During my breakup, there were people who actually thought I was having a mental breakdown.

They believed—and they actually *said*—that I must have been mentally unhinged to have allowed my relationship to fall through my fingers. This was not only hurtful, it just simply wasn't true. I wouldn't allow myself to dwell on it too much otherwise it would have just made me angry; however, it became laughable to me that just because I was doing what was best for myself (and not anyone else) for the first time in my life that it must have been because I was having a breakdown of sorts. That couldn't have been further from the truth. I still give a mental middle finger to those people today: Thanks for the support, assholes.

There were others—other mouths who spoke and other eyes who saw what they thought was the truth—who actually thought I was having an affair. These were the people who needed a reason that would justify (in their own minds) the rationale for such a breakup. They needed a reason that would excuse (or at least explain) why I would leave the charmed life I'd been living for the past nine years.

All I had to say to those people was that not everything was always as it seemed, and I hadn't been okay for a while, and I was doing what was best for myself even if it wasn't what was best for others. I remained true to myself and true to my tribe, which for me, then, needed to be a tribe of which I was the primary...scratch that...the *sole* member.

A few words of caution as it concerns how to react when people first hear the news about your breakup: Remember that when it all boils down to it, it's no one's business but your own.

It was so much easier telling people I hardly knew that I was separated or divorcing. It was almost like practice because I didn't really care about these people. It was terrible to have to tell my family (especially my parents and my siblings) because I felt like I was letting them down. I'd always, *always* been the glue that held everyone together and now I was falling apart. It was my job to be *okay* for them, and I felt like I had failed.

Telling friends was just as bad. Some of them responded in such a kind and caring way. Others would listen in shock, then avoid me like the plague—as if divorce was a contagious disease that might somehow be caught by them. They wanted nothing more to do with me.

Some would even suggest that maybe I hadn't done enough to prevent it from happening—I hadn't tried hard enough or fought fiercely enough to save what we had. The judgments and opinions would fly at me, fast and furious. It was shocking to me that people who I thought would be there for me *disappeared.* However, the friends I had who stepped up really stepped up for me in a big way. Instead of making me feel judged, they made me feel loved.

Just loved.

Everyone will have different reactions to your news. It will be helpful to tell those who you think will be supportive first... and then once you feel more fully healed, then others can know.

Unfortunately, though, this kind of careful orchestration isn't always possible, especially since the world is so steeped in the immediacy and forced intimacy of social media. When it comes to "other eyes," we must, finally, face Facebook, Instagram, Twitter, the list goes on and on. In this day and age, really, a breakup doesn't involve two people, but potentially millions. (Facebook has a "divorced" profile option, for God's sake!)

Privacy in today's world is almost an anomaly. We have completely redefined what it is. Everyone, absolutely everyone, knows about the status of our relationships, our engagements, the success (or failure) of our marriages, the births of our babies, the deaths of our loved ones. You can't avoid it when you are going through a tough time.

When it comes to announcing or dealing with the news of your breakup on social media, you can go about it in two ways: You can respectfully disappear for a while during the worst of it and then come back when you are ready, or you can go the route I did (probably not recommended) and keep posting as though everything is *fine, fine, fine.*

Until one day you are like, *Uh, I am not actually fine…*

I guess it all goes back to that pattern of perfection I fought so hard to uphold earlier in my life—the pattern I've written about in earlier chapters that keeps coming up to bite me in the ass.

During my divorce, I kept up my social media postings as if everything was, well, *perfect* (that awful word again). But eventually people noticed that I sounded "different" in my posts and began making comments that were not very kind. People had to weigh in. I was very public with my marriage on TV and on social media. How did I expect my divorce to suddenly be private? Naiveté, I guess?

The problem, of course, is that people on social media can

become very opinionated and vocal during a difficult time when you just don't need that in your life—you're already in enough pain. And they can get fucking *mean.*

When that happened, I adopted a pretty nasty *fuck-you* attitude toward it all, which I'm not sure was the best way to be. In fact, none of this would have been an issue if I had just stopped posting altogether during this difficult time. I should have closed up shop, shut things down, at least until the storm had subsided. But I was too busy trying to appear perfect, to create the image that everything was just fine. Even when it clearly wasn't.

But herein lies another life lesson: That warped pattern of perfection could have followed me throughout my entire life, but I had sense enough, eventually, to cut it out. I refused to let it follow me.

Sure, I stayed on Facebook and Instagram a little longer than I should have, but in doing so, I learned a valuable lesson: Keep your own business your own business. Resist the urge to post every detail because it throws you off your game and distracts you from what you should actually be working on— which is your real self and your real problems.

Learn to say fuck it and walk away from not only your postings but from the insatiable desire to be perfect all the time. It took some time, but I did it. It took some time, but I finally got it right.

I'm glad I can look back on it now and realize my mistakes. We live and we learn, right? When it comes to other's eyes, and the well-meaning and not-so-well-meaning advice, remember to remain true to yourself. Through it all, listen to that voice within because it will never steer you wrong.

To trust yourself, you must know yourself, though. This means developing the tools to let go of all the life preservers that everyone is throwing at you from their position of safety on the shoreline and giving yourself the freedom to float, by yourself, in the deep water. This means giving yourself permission to arrive at solutions armed with all you have in your heart, rather than using the empty advice of those who might love you but have no idea of what you are facing.

When others rush to speak out on your behalf, quiet their voices and listen to the only one that matters: the voice within.

It will take time, but this much I know is true, because it worked for me. Getting to that place of self-trust is difficult, not impossible. Though it might be a long haul, it's a haul worth making. It is a trek. But trust me on this:

You can get there on your own.

"Know thyself."

—Socrates

CHAPTER SEVEN
LEARNING TO SURF

"Sometimes, in the waves of change, we find our true direction."

—*Unknown*

*I*f you are about to bear the brunt of a breakup or if you find yourself standing face-to-face with the daunting prospect of divorce, you're going to need to hold on to something that will help you survive. Something to keep you afloat. Something to give you balance and buoyancy when the waters get rough and the waves get high.

For me, it was surfing.

I took my first surfing lesson right after the split. Both literally and figuratively, I felt like I was sinking, fighting to breathe, tangled up underwater, and I needed something to pull me out of my deep-water depression.

Surfing is what saved me.

I remember that first lesson like it was yesterday, although sometimes I wish I didn't.

The instructor pulled up with a bunch of brightly colored surfboards piled high in the back of his truck. It was a pretty windy day, and although I thought the waves looked gigantic, I am positive as I look back on the memory today those waves were only knee height. (See how your perspective expands over time and stretches out with experience?)

While standing on the beach, we practiced popping up on the boards as the instructor talked about what we'd do when we got into the water. I remember thinking, *Wait, we get in the water on the first lesson? Shouldn't we be, like, I don't know, stretching in the sand?* I wanted to object, but there was something about this stranger with the surfboards with his shaggy blonde hair and clear blue eyes; he had a calming effect on me, and I felt like I could trust him—so into the water I went.

It seemed too much, too soon. Even though I'd basically grown up going to Virginia Beach during just about every summer of my childhood, I'd still been terrified of the ocean even then—crazy, I know, but that was simply the reality of the situation. Whatever the case and whatever my history, here was the long and short of the situation on that first day: I was fucking scared.

I remember getting into the ocean in my newly purchased wetsuit, board in tow (an embarrassingly large, blue and white striped foam board), but what I remember most about that moment was the feeling of pure and complete panic.

Panic.

If I'm being honest here, I don't remember all that much about being in the water. Sheer terror will cause you to forget things. I might have stood up on the board a time or two? Maybe? I do remember that during the last set, the waves crashed hard over my head and I literally climbed up on the instructor's back, probably scratching his eyes out in the process. (Apologies to him, a story I'm sure he still tells to this day—actually, I *know* he still tells this story.) Once back on dry land, he was convinced he'd lost me as a student for good (I know because he told me as much later that summer).

He obviously didn't know who he was dealing with.

Little did he know that I was determined to master the skill and to survive the highest waves because my mind and my body and my life depended on it. *I needed to learn to stay afloat—especially when the waves were at their highest.*

I'll never forget that day—the anxiety of it all, the feeling of helplessness and panic. It related totally and completely to the life I was leading then. It was precisely what I needed in that moment, though I didn't realize it at the time because it certainly didn't feel like what I needed as I was bobbing around in that vast ocean, trying to find my balance. But I needed it. I needed something to make me feel alive, even if it terrified me.

That's what surfing did for me. It connected me back to myself. It made me feel whole again, even if life all around me was falling apart and disconnecting at just about every level you could imagine. It provided light where there was only darkness before.

In fact, surfing and being in the ocean (my "happy place," I always call it) was the only thing that pulled me out of my own darkness. It was the only time during the split when I was truly happy, the only place I would smile. Because I didn't have control over the ocean, I *had* to pay attention or else I would get smashed by a wave.

I was laughing and focused when I was in the water. I couldn't sink into my own grief when I was out there. It was amazing, unlike anything I'd ever felt before. Once I had gotten over the fear, the joy was what remained—the joy of playing and laughing like I honestly hadn't played and laughed in years.

I was constantly smiling when I was my board. It always felt like I was flying. Even when I was *falling*, I was laughing. I felt so alive in the bright sunshine, so alive and real and happy in that sea of sparkling water. In my happy memories of that summer, on that ocean, there is always a glittering blue sheen on the water.

I realize, of course, not everyone can just put down this book and go learn how to surf if you're going through a breakup or a hard time in a relationship. It's not possible, realistic, or advisable.

What *is* possible and what *is* realistic, though, is for me to share some of the lessons I learned back then that stay with me to this day. I share them now in the hope that you can incorporate at least some of the lessons' wisdom into your own daily rhythm. Short of a surfboard (although I do have a few extras if you need them), I offer you this:

SURFING LESSON #1: I needed to face my fears. Two things I hated most, the two things that created the most fear in my heart, were a lack of control and the vastness of the ocean, the unknown. The ocean itself forced me to face *both* of these fears, simultaneously.

THE LIFE LESSON: Try something new that scares the fucking hell out of you. If nothing else, it will be a good and necessary distraction from the pain you are going through.

SURFING LESSON #2: Surrender to the fact that you have to completely give up control when you're on (and in) the ocean. The ocean is unpredictable and all you can control is your reaction to it.

THE LIFE LESSON: Stop trying to control everything. When you are going through a breakup, the only things you can control are yourself and your reactions—and sometimes even controlling those things feels impossible. But it is not.

SURFING LESSON #3: Pay attention. If you don't, you're going to get smacked in the face—hard!—by either the wave or the board. Or both.

THE LIFE LESSON: Pay attention to your life as it unfolds. Don't let it just *happen* to you. You are the driver here. Don't let too much time pass without taking a quick inventory of the decisions you're making and the actions you're taking. It's all-too-easy to become numb for a while, and although that's okay for a minute, it's *not* okay forever.

SURFING LESSON #4: Laugh, laugh, laugh like hell when you catch a great wave. Laugh when you get knocked on your ass. Laugh. Smile. Cry. Have fun.

THE LIFE LESSON: What you are going through is serious—the shake-up of a lifetime. But please, don't forget to have fun, don't forget to laugh at yourself during the good times and the bad. Otherwise, what's the point in all of this "working on yourself" stuff?

SURFING LESSON #5: You've got to learn to relax on that board—otherwise you will fall. Plain and simple.

THE LIFE LESSON: If you don't relax your grip, you'll *lose* your grip at some point.

SURFING LESSON #6: Whenever you fall, cover your face. This is the first thing they teach you.

THE LIFE LESSON: To be completely honest, I'm not sure how this one translates to real life, which is okay, too. I just knew I didn't want to end up with a broken nose, a concussion, or a black eye from my board. So just cover your face, okay?

I'm sure that spending a summer surfing with a big group of vagabond men might not have been the best thing for my public "image." (If I was worried about that kind of thing; maybe I should have been? But this is no time for regrets.)

However, once I stopped giving a shit about what others thought of me, I started truly living. That group of guys I surfed with didn't care who I was, where I came from, or my "current relationship status." What they *did* care about was showing me that the ocean could be a very healing place.

We had sunrise surfing sessions, picnics on the beach, midnight bonfires, talking about nothing at all and laughing at everything. They taught me to really *take hold* of life and do anything I needed to do to be happy—even if it was considered selfish. As a result, I developed a tougher shell because I *had to* in order to survive.

The Summer of the Split, the summer of my surfing lessons, *I stopped asking permission to live and just did what I wanted.* When do we ever let ourselves just do that? That summer, to be sure, was easily the best and the worst of my life.

Helping out at a surf camp for kids also created a healing, happy place for me. Being around them was a real eye-opener. They were just so excited and happy—even when they were scared! Even when they were being knocked down by those giant waves.

They'd just shake it off and go right back. Shake it off and try again. Shake it off and climb back on to the board. It was pretty incredible to see those little lives in the ocean. They should have been terrified, but for some reason, they were immune to it. They didn't know terror.

And after that summer, I no longer knew it either. At least not in the way I used to know it. My relationship with terror had been forever changed.

I want to close this chapter with a blog I wrote some time ago about my brother. It has to do with surfing, with survival, and with simply living life. Hopefully, his wisdom will help you now as much as it helped me then:

I spoke to my brother this morning and even though he's in his twenties—and my baby brother—sometimes he can be wise beyond his years.

The last time I talked to him I told him about my trip to Costa Rica in April and how I had a pretty bad scare while surfing. I went headlong over the edge of a wave, got thrown around, and ended up with the leash of my surfboard caught around my neck. I had a moment of "I'm not coming up from this" that ended when I slammed into the sand—probably because I thought I was going to break my neck.

I haven't had many surfing incidents that have truly scared me—but this one threw me for a loop—literally and figuratively. I refused to catch a wave after that and swam in…pretty shaken up but too proud to admit it. I haven't been in the water since, and I've been telling myself it's because I haven't had the time.

I didn't think too much about the whole story while I was telling it to my brother over the weekend—he had asked me when I was in the water last and I told him about it. Today when we spoke, I forgot that I had even said anything.

We spent time catching up this morning and before we got off the phone he stopped abruptly and goes, "Do me a favor." I figured he needed something, and so I paused in saying goodbye, when he continued with, "Don't forget what it felt like that time you caught your first wave."

I was confused by what he said at first and then realized he was going back to my Costa Rica surf story. He continued with, "You're probably scared now…but don't forget what that first wave felt like. That high…remember it."

Maybe in his head he was just telling me to get back out there on a surfboard, but little did he know his advice would carry into so many facets of life and was so helpful to hear this morning. I'll have it running through my head all week…maybe a little longer.

How often do we let fear hold us back from giving it our all? How often do we let fear run our lives? Getting scared when we do something a little tough because we might not succeed—or not trying again when something goes wrong.

Don't let fear hold you back from feeling the high. Try again, because the high is worth it.

The high is more than worth it…

*

I'll remember my brother's words for the rest of my life, and the wisdom he shared with me then is worthy of my sharing with you now.

When I think back to those days now, I smile inside because I now realize that, through those darkest days, the water was my light.

To this day, being in the ocean is still my happy place. Surfing turned me into a mermaid, or if not a mermaid, at least a better version of myself. I will never be afraid of the ocean again because it taught me (and continues to teach me) so much about myself.

*"You cannot stop the waves,
but you can learn to surf."*

—Jon Kabat-Zin

CHAPTER EIGHT
THE SELF-LOVE PROJECT

"Because at this moment, the only one deserving of your love is you. It's time to take the love that others take for granted and invest it into yourself."

—R.H. Sin

*W*hy is it that we forget to love ourselves? Why do we so often leave that love behind—right at the time when we need it most? When crisis and chaos step directly into the center of our lives, why can't we be kind to ourselves long enough to find our breath and our balance again?

The sad truth is most women facing broken relationships have lost their sense of self-love *long* before the relationship begins to buckle. We've either misplaced it or it has misplaced us. Walked away. Gone AWOL. Never to be seen or heard from again.

I write this chapter to bring that love back.

In order to bring it back, though, we need to figure out why it left in the first place. My theories are based on my own personal experience. They stem straight from my own heart. And I share them because they saved me then—and maybe they can save you now. It is straight talk for women whose hearts are hurting and who have forgotten, somewhere along the way, how to love themselves.

There are more of us out there than you think.

The picture we paint is heart-wrenching and familiar. We tend to want to fix everything. Everything except ourselves. For this reason, when a relationship is broken beyond the point of repair, we tend to stay in it anyway, thinking we can fix it. Patch it up. Make it right. By the time it's over, we are so incredibly broken that the thought of "fixing" or loving ourselves has become a completely foreign concept, a distant dream.

So we place the blame on ourselves. We become the victim (and I can't think of anything less empowering than that). We ask ourselves questions that are self-defeating and filled with guilt. *What could I have done differently? Why did we split? What part of this breakup was because of me? Where did I go wrong? Should I have done more? Tried harder?*

With these questions come certain sensations, deep, disturbing sensations, which throw us even more off-center. We feel sad, ugly, unloved. We continue to blame ourselves. And here is the most vicious part of the cycle that we don't see coming until after it's knocked us to the ground: Before we know it, we're riding a downward spiral that doesn't end until we hit bottom. Hard.

Here is what I consider to be the happy news in the midst of all of this sadness. Here is the redemptive message. Here is the news that will put you back in the driver's seat, give you back your control and put you back on the path to self-love. Listen carefully...

You are the only one who can stop your own downward spiral. You are the only one who can learn to love yourself again. It's got to be you.

No therapist, no friend, no family member, and no well-meaning stranger on the street is going to teach you how to love yourself again. You are the only one who can do that. Sure, they can *tell* you to start loving yourself again. They can offer up tips and techniques that might have worked for them. They can serve you cookie-cutter, formulaic, this-is-what-worked-for-me solutions—bullshit wrapped up in silver bows—but the only one who's actually going to get you back on your journey toward self-love is you.

Just you.

Chances are you won't discover this renewed sense of self-love while you're at bottom. Self-love rarely exists there. But if you're reading this from a low and hopeless place, if your bottom has risen up to meet you and you feel like there's no place else you can turn, I'm here to tell you that I've been there. I've been in that place of self-hatred. It was dark and painful.

But do not despair because here is the honest truth. I've said this before, and it has become a mindful mantra and a constant theme throughout this book: The *bottom* of our own downward spiral is where we sometimes need to be. It's where we learn the most about ourselves. It can give us the momentum we need to redirect our trajectory and return, again, to a place of satisfaction and self-love.

There is beauty at the bottom. Even though it hurts like hell, being there is sometimes a necessary part of the process. Facing our weakest selves—our darkest, broken-down, beaten-up, trampled-on selves—will get us back to where we need to be. Being there (not indefinitely or forever, mind you, but for only a period of time) teaches us that we are strong and can get through anything life will throw at us in the future.

Hitting bottom is a very personal process. Mine is different than yours. Your saturation point, your buckling point, your darkest moment, is different than mine. *Whatever* that bottom looks like, whatever it feels like (and I guarantee you it will not feel pleasant), belongs to you and you alone. It isn't something you should avoid…but it's also not something you should stay stuck in for any longer than you have to.

Here's what I feel about being at your bottom: It isn't a place you want to set down roots and call home. But as temporary housing, it has the potential to change your life forever (for the better) if you let it.

I guess what I'm saying is that forgetting how to love yourself might create all kinds of personal pain, but as long as you come out on the other side, as long as you bring yourself *back* eventually, to a place of love and understanding, your pain will at least have counted for something. In a very real way, the depth of your own pain will be what holds the potential to push you toward growth.

Finding self-love when you're in the middle of a failing relationship is virtually impossible. I know because I lost every single ounce of self-love when I was the middle of my own breakup. But the actual truth of the matter is this: When anger, shock, and anxiety are all around you, when depression and sadness have all but immobilized your body and knocked you on your ass, learning to love yourself again is the only thing that will allow you to get up, shake it off, and keep on moving.

Self-love is the only thing that will save you.

For better or for worse, self-love was something I was never particularly good at. It was not an instinctive act. What *was* instinctive, as I've mentioned before, was my driving desire to please others and put other people's needs before my own. I'd neglect myself to the point where it would actually become scary, running myself into the ground to help others while ignoring the person who should have been the most important in the world to me: myself.

Even writing these words right now makes me sad because it's a reminder of the person I used to be—the people-pleasing person who never put herself first and who never really even liked herself that much. The sad-inside person who was busy trying to prove to the outside world that she was *fine, fine, fine*.

I wasn't just bad at this self-love thing when I was in a relationship, oh no. This was basically me, my entire life... until now. When I was younger, it didn't catch up to me, not in any aggressive sense at least, until I was just out of college and had landed my first job in fashion.

I was the assistant to the director of PR at a large, successful company, but I had the boss from hell. I swear you couldn't even make up the kind of stuff I went through. I was stressed 24/7 and horribly unhappy in that work environment.

The only time I'd make for myself was in the evening, when I'd go to the gym for a workout. I guess looking back on it, I could say that going to gym watching my caloric intake, and counting my carbs like crazy actually *started out* as a form of self-love and self-preservation. I had to find a way to maintain some sense of normalcy and sanity, so off to the gym I went.

It started out as a way to escape the pain and frustration I was feeling at work, and it provided the only sense of control I could find at the time. My mentality was to try to control the world around me. To stay ahead of the game. To push myself beyond my capacity, please my boss from hell at any cost, and make everything all right again.

But that dream very quickly turned into a nightmare.

Each day, the nightmare grew worse. I started starving myself and working out *too* much. At the same time, my boss had become so verbally abusive, demanding, and erratic that it was hard to keep my balance.

It's probably the closest thing to a nervous breakdown I've ever experienced.

Looking back, I'm not sure I'd describe what I had as a full-blown eating disorder but more of a *control* issue. Whenever my life felt like it was getting out of control—which was all the time, back then—I'd turn to the only thing I *could* control, which was food and working out. It turned into an ugly and frightening extreme.

I'd hit my bottom.

Mistakenly, I thought I was showing myself self-love during this difficult time, but all I was doing was starving myself and working out too much. Where is the self-love in *that?*

I couldn't continue on the track I was on. I was hungry, exhausted, and miserable all the time. I was losing myself and losing my grip. So I quit my job and moved back home to Virginia for a few months, back to the farm of my childhood.

Back to my roots.

Was it embarrassing having to head home with my tail between my legs? Absolutely. But it was something I needed to do to learn to love myself again. It was my necessary rock bottom...

I'd forgotten how to take care of myself. How to love myself. How to put myself first and treat myself with dignity and respect. Those are things that, at twenty-three or twenty-four years old, you can't afford to forget. So what did I do?

I went home to remember.

I had some bad, bad days while I was back home on the farm. But, eventually, those bad days slowly turned to good days. My parents and my brother (who was home and in high school at the time) were obviously very concerned. They knew I was broken, and it hurt them to see me this way.

Looking back on it now, I realize how much it took for them to just let me ride it out. To just let me walk through it. They let me do what I needed to do to get better and tap into that place of self-love again that had all but disappeared. Did I ever thank them for that? If I didn't then, I need to now: *Thank you, family, for letting me find myself again and for embracing me when I needed you most.*

I thought a lot about things while I was home. Worked through a lot of issues (or at least I thought I did, until they came back to bite me in the ass again during my marriage). I wrote a lot. Reflected a lot. Read a lot. Began to embrace the imbalances in my life for exactly what they were—imbalances. And then one day, after I'd been home for a bit, I looked at my family and just said, "It's time for me to move back to New York City."

I realize now how hard it was for them to let me move back and let go of me again. But for me, a large part of my own self-love was tied to my independence, and I knew the fact that I was ready to return meant, slowly but surely, my sense of self was returning, too.

Hitting my bottom gave me enough positive momentum to change my own trajectory. By falling so deep, and by hitting so hard, I was able to eventually change direction and begin the climb back up. I was able to begin the journey toward learning to love myself again. So hitting bottom was what actually helped bring my balance back.

What's ironic and very revealing here is that my first real "bottom"—my first real downward spiral toward depression and away from self-love—occurred as a result of my relationship with *myself,* rather than a romantic relationship with someone else, which proves my point perfectly: Your relationship with yourself creates the foundation for all else. It is the basis for your joy, but also for your pain, for your sense of balance and control but also for your sense of loss and, yes, even self-abuse (or at least self-anguish). It's simple, really: It all starts with *you.*

Since your relationship with yourself is kind of the key to everything, you might expect me to say something at this point about the importance of staying true to yourself, even in times of trouble. But that would be bullshit, really, because you don't really *know* who you are at the time…so how can you be true to it?

You are in the midst of breaking open, of tearing apart, of discovering some new, essential part of yourself that you might not have even met before, and you just don't know how (or if) all the pieces are going to fit back together. Staying true to something that is newly emerging is difficult, if not impossible. And definitely not advisable.

What you *can* do, however, if you can't be true to yourself during a tumultuous time, is at least be *kind* to yourself. This is when the self-love will flow back in. This is where you treat yourself with kindness, with kid gloves, and with a sense of caring and compassion.

During this time, you can also try to bring your balance back. Right after my breakup, balance was not something I was interested in. Sitting in the middle of my own excess and my own extremes felt more comfortable. I did some things I'm not particularly proud of.

I'll just admit it. During that time, I flirted a little too often, kissed people I shouldn't have, drank a little too much, never realizing—at least not then—that those things weren't going to make me feel better about myself. When it boils down to it (and only today can I say this with clarity and conviction), those were forms of self-hatred, not self-love. They were distractions.

It's important to remember that there is a difference between arrogance and self-love. Self-love, in its most genuine form, is doing things for yourself that no one else might ever see; you're the only beneficiary and often the only witness.

Arrogance, on the other hand, is something that you want others to see. It's self-serving in a negative way. A distraction that serves no purpose other than to make you feel better in the short-term and position you in a positive light to the outside world. It will not help you get back on the path to truly loving yourself. I can say this with an honest heart because arrogance was also a part of my journey.

Taking myself out to a nice dinner "just because"—that was self-love. Posting a sexy photo of myself on my Instagram, you could say that was self-love, but it really was arrogance. It wasn't me being confident and loving myself, it was me showing everyone that I was "okay" going through my breakup and, dammit, I looked good doing it.

It was almost like I needed the gratification of social media to show the world I was the best at getting divorced (that old perfection cycle showing itself again). I was skinny and fit, I was blonde, I was going out at night, I could now show my body off without worrying about disapproving eyes telling me what I could and couldn't post.

This was not me genuinely loving myself; this was me being an asshole. Hell, maybe I *needed* to be that asshole for a minute in order to come full circle. In order to truly cycle back to myself. But still, I knew it wasn't healing me. It was just my own arrogance merely protecting me from feeling the hurt and pain I needed to feel at that time. Sure, I could lie to myself and call it self-love, but it was really a distraction and a defense mechanism. Nothing more and nothing less.

Eventually, though, through hard work, soul-searching therapy, and a driving desire to change the direction of my toxic trajectory, I was able to get through that storm of self-doubt, arrogance, and self-abuse. I put myself on a path that would bring me back to myself, back to the Kris who loved herself enough to want to find her center again, even if her center had somehow been altered or modified.

Here's a list of loving steps I took after my own breakup. These are things that helped me learn to love (and *like*) myself again. Maybe your list will look different, but I urge you to try to create one for yourself anyway.

STEPPING BACK INTO SELF-LOVE

JOURNALING: I've kept a journal my entire life. Sometimes I'll share those feelings in my blog, as a way to heal and to share with others. To this day, I go back and read my old journal entries as a reminder of how far I've come and how far I've yet to go.

SURFING: Surfing taught me how to trust myself again, how to let go, and how to celebrate the fact that it's sometimes okay to wipe out.

WORKING OUT/FITNESS: This is a must for me. I have to have some kind of fitness in my daily routine in order to feel motivated, connected, and mentally *okay.*

READING: As a girl, I was quiet and very shy, and also able to get through a book or two a day. I loved getting lost in the story. Even today, I still make the time to read. Every single day.

COOKING FOR MYSELF: I love trying out new dishes and cooking for myself. Some people might hate it, but cooking and baking are like therapy for me.

DINING SOLO: Feeling blue or angry or overwhelmed? Try slipping out to a new neighborhood restaurant. Even today, I use this time to recharge. There's something anchoring and refreshing about being lost in your thoughts while eating something that you love...alone.

GET A NEW LOOK: I went from brunette to blonde during my separation and it just made me feel different, like another person. Making time for the small, superficial stuff—nails, hair, maybe even a tattoo—are small things that might make a big difference. Have fun with this one.

BE SOCIAL: Being friendly and chatting with strangers is one of my favorite things to do. I love talking to people, finding out about the things in their lives that make them happy and learning about pieces of their story. I joined a public library so I could browse new books and have somewhere to go daily to be around new people if I wanted to. And I'd visit my neighborhood coffee shop every single morning, not just for the coffee but to talk to people. It helped get me out of bed each day.

TRAVEL: More on this in a coming chapter, but getting up and getting out is a great way to learn to love yourself—and rediscover yourself!—all over again. Plan a little adventure or a quick getaway. It doesn't have to be exotic or expensive. Self-love is about making time for yourself, and travel is a great way to do that!

Today, happily, I'd say that my list is still pretty much the same. Everything on it represents my own "recovery" from my split, and as someone who has never been all that great with finding self-love or putting myself first, it's important that I don't lose this piece of myself ever again.

Never again.

*

Finally, as I close this chapter, I want to share this letter I wrote—possibly to a younger version of myself, or possibly to someone who is holding this book and looking for some guidance, someone who's just in need of some sisterly or motherly advice.

For you:

As women, we are constantly criticizing ourselves. You will experience this a lot in your lifetime, and I can't say that I truly know how to protect you. But I want to tell you things about me—the good and the not-so-good— as a way to prevent you from making the same mistakes I made. Or maybe you'll need to make those mistakes to learn, to grow, to be real.

You will need to know independence and how to take care of yourself, and I will remind you, always, that you don't need anyone to do anything for you. You've got this. I will teach you that, although you might find someone who will compliment and magnify your happiness, you can be happy and whole on your own. You can create your own happiness.

I will teach you to love yourself on good days and bad days and to be easy on and gentle with yourself at all times. I'll teach you to ask for help when you really need it and to avoid taking on every single project solo.

I will teach you that the number on your bathroom scale doesn't define your self-worth, that being strong is more important than being skinny, and that you must tell yourself every single day that you are beautiful.

Most importantly, I will teach you what I think I know best: You should be kind to every person you come across in this world, even if you don't like them all that much, because you must always be kind. Always. And that kindness shouldn't just be reserved for others, but for you, too.

Self-love is a combination of so many things: independence, kindness, trusting your intuition, knowing your worth; being able to speak up, stand up, claim your space in this world; and lastly (and most importantly), it's choosing on a daily basis to see the positives in life. It's choosing to be happy.

Keep loving yourself, no matter what. You deserve your love. You need your love. And you are the only one who can give yourself the love you truly deserve.

xo,

Kris

"You yourself, as much as anybody in the entire universe, deserve your love and affection."

—Buddha

CHAPTER NINE

HEALTH IS HAPPINESS

"I have chosen to be happy because it is good for my health."

—Voltaire

I see it clearly now—the pattern.

It's a pattern I used to have but today no longer own. It's a pattern that owned *me*, really—it took up residence in my head and pushed me around for much of my adult life. It was, as I've mentioned before, a life of extremes, of perpetual imbalance. Moderation was elusive. Imbalance felt better.

So often (more often than I care to admit), my footing felt tentative and unsure, like I was climbing up the side of a very steep mountain. I did my best to appear sure-footed and confident to the outside world, but inside it felt like I was climbing up Mt. Everest…without a harness.

It was not a healthy way to live.

Maybe I'd moderate for a little while, find a comfortable rhythm, but invariably something would happen that would knock things out of whack. When that happened—whether it was an unpleasant job, an unhealthy friendship, or the eventual dissolution of my own marriage—unhealthy patterns would begin to surface.

And when that balance was compromised, staying healthy was no longer my top priority. Staying *alive* was.

During the Summer of the Split, healthy living, healthy thinking, and healthy behavior were not really front-and-center (or even a blip) on my radar screen. I never understood it when people would say to me they were too sad to eat...until it happened to me.

I literally lost my appetite for everything. When I lost ten pounds, I used to joke about my "divorce abs." I realize now, of course, that it wasn't funny at all. It was really fucking sad.

I was really fucking sad.

I wasn't as balanced as I could have been about it—nothing in my life was really balanced during that time—but getting up and getting to the gym as often as I did really ended up being my salvation. My salvation that was sometimes a curse in my life.

Funny how things work out because today the gym is my happy place.

When I was married, and for much of my adult life, I'd go to the gym daily, typically exhausted, always maintaining a very strict diet that didn't allow me to have fun dinners or even the occasional pleasure of a cheat day. To put it quite simply, I ran myself into the ground. I didn't make myself or my true health a priority.

I was constantly stressed out, running around non-stop, anxious, and forever preoccupied with maintaining a strict schedule because that's what I expected of myself. I saw the picture of my own health and well-being through a clouded lens. Sadly, that picture, even through my own eyes, looked distant and abstract because I thought I was fine—fine and healthy.

There was nothing healthy about it.

The saddest and the scariest part of all, though, was how well I deluded myself into thinking that I was okay, that I knew my limits, that I had everything under control and would eventually, after this "hiccup" was over (whatever it might have been), get back to being my typically happy, optimistic self. All this empty, baseless, *I'm-gonna-be-okay* bravado should have been a warning sign that I was not okay, of course...but I was too blind to see it. I was too delusional to see the truth: I was not okay at all.

In fact, now that I'm looking back on it, when it came to healthy living, I never really sat in the middle of that moderation road in my younger years, either. In my early twenties, "being fit" was all about a number on a scale and how many days a week I was killing myself at the gym. It's a negative pattern—a destructive cycle—that women too often fall into without realizing they're even in it until it's too late. I was in it, deep in it.

I was caught up in that cycle. Trapped in my own toxicity, without even realizing I was poisoning my own system. And while I was in it, I felt like I was the only one there. The solo sufferer. The invisible, lonely girl who exercised too much, ate too little, and really didn't know what healthy living really was.

Today I realize I was not alone. Other women were suffering right along with me, trapped in the throes of their own grief, just expressing it in different ways and under the mistaken impression that they, too, were all alone. It's amazing, really, and not in a good way, how unhealthy living can cause us to put our blinders on and just run straight ahead—toward what, exactly? I'm not sure any of us really know because I do not believe we are running toward true happiness.

The blessing in looking back, of course, is the realization that I was *never* really alone, even though it sure felt like I was at the time. Others were suffering in many of the same ways I was. Plus, I was too busy helping others and too busy making sure that everybody else was okay that I forgot to remember to take care of myself. Too often, we forget about ourselves. And we forget we are not alone in our grief.

When that happens, our health takes a back seat. Our happiness takes a back seat. We take a back seat to *ourselves* and allow the needs of others to drive us in everything we do. It's a familiar, age-old, ancient pattern (*rut* is probably a better word), and my goal here is to take that destructive cycle and break it down. Bring it to a graceful conclusion so that we can get back to the business of getting healthy again and creating positive, forward-moving patterns in our daily lives.

If we don't move forward, we will continue to suffer. And here I should probably be more direct. If *you* don't, you'll languish and leave behind the most precious commodity of all: yourself.

When it comes to easing someone else's pain, especially if they're facing the fury that comes with closing a relationship, we *can* help each other heal. It might not be with I-told-you-so advice or stay-away-from-that-asshole guidance—it might not even be guidance at *all*—but we can still try to help each other heal.

We don't have to suffer alone.

In fact, from this point forward, especially as it concerns your mental and physical health, you should now have this mantra: *Although I must find and decide the solutions on my own, I never have to feel alone in my grief again. There are others out there who are suffering, too, and that knowledge, if nothing else, pulls me back from the brink of isolation. I am not alone.*

How can I make this bold statement with such clarity and conviction? Because I was at that brink of that same isolation and despair myself. I know what it feels like. And because I know the pain that comes from living in the middle of such extremes, I need to send the message now to those of you who might be sitting in the middle of your own messiness at this very moment, because it's why I wanted to write this book: You are not alone.

You are not alone.

Even if it feels like you're the only other person whose health is suffering, whose balance is off, whose relationship with food and exercise and healthy eating during this difficult time (or other times in your life) has been dangerously compromised, remember that others are going through it right alongside you. You're not the first person to go through a breakup, and you won't be the last.

Maybe they're not going through it *with* you, because everyone is facing their own challenges in their own ways, but they're walking right beside you. Right at this very moment. For this reason alone, we can and should do whatever we can to provide each other a little sweet, simple relief.

I urge you to, as the philosopher Rumi says, *"Be a lamp, or a lifeboat, or a ladder. Help someone's soul heal."*

Each of us has the capacity, when it comes to our own healing, to also help someone else heal in the process. Even if helping others is not the primary intention, it is often the pleasant byproduct. In a very real sense, as it is often said, healed people heal people.

I know this was true in my case.

For me, writing this book has been a healing journey. It has soothed my spirit and softened some of the still-razor-sharp edges of pain that I'd convinced myself had all but disappeared but actually had not. It has also given me the opportunity to recognize and celebrate not only the positive lifestyle patterns that have led me to a healthier place but also the people behind those patterns. There is a human element to healing, too.

Pilates, in fact, was the one thing that really helped me heal during the worst stages of my breakup. This gave me a reason to wake up every day.

But it was also the incredible woman who introduced me to Pilates, who really acted as the ladder and the lamp for me. She really did help me through some of the toughest times. By introducing me to the technique, and by being present and available to take me through the steps each day, she became a kind of lifeboat. So, the practice as well as the person were my ladders out of grief.

I had practiced Pilates in the past but didn't really fall in love with it until the Summer of the Split. The thing with Pilates is that you *have* to slow down and pay close attention to your body. It's not about lifting the heaviest weight, running the fastest mile, or upping your heart rate to a new high. It's not about the group effort or the calorie burn. It's simply about you. Just you.

It's about listening to your breath, paying attention to your core, and being mindful of the moments that you create while you're in them. Let me tell you this: All of this is very hard to do when you're sad. But by doing them, by creating these moments and focusing on your breath and your core rather than on your sadness, the sadness itself is forced to take a back seat. There's no more room for it.

Very quickly, Pilates became a positive pattern in my life. A healthy habit. It was something that wouldn't beat my body up even if I was doing it five or six times a week. Both the practice *and* the pattern began to shine a bright, new light into my darkness, a light that not only strengthened my core and toned my body but also taught me to slow the hell *down*. To become more mindful. To breathe in, settle down, and turn inward to find that peaceful place inside my brain that slowed my mind and evened me out.

Seeing my Pilates instructor in the mornings gave me a reason to get out of bed. On the days I knew I was going to see her, I'd wake up excited and ready to start my day. Excited to practice my technique. To push my body to new heights without pushing it to dangerous extremes. Pilates gave me power. It gave me a reason to connect with myself. It made me feel whole again.

This healthy pattern helped turn my life around in a moment when I really needed it.

Eventually, I came to love my mornings again, just like I used to. When things were good, mornings were my favorite time. I'd wake up, make myself coffee, turn on the *Today* show, and eat my breakfast of oatmeal and peanut butter while reading the news online. That, to me, was peace—the one point in the day when it was okay for me to slow down and not rush anywhere.

But when my split happened, my mornings became my misery. I'd have the hardest time getting up and the hardest time greeting a new day. I couldn't eat breakfast. I'd go out for coffee just because I was so desperate for the human interaction.

Today, my health cycle has come full circle, probably because *I myself* have come full circle. My health regimen today is far more holistic, far less extreme. It is more balanced... because I am far more balanced.

Today, being fit means eating balanced meals because that's

what makes me *feel good*. It means lifting weights and getting strong to stay healthy…not to get skinny. It means taking days off when I know I need to, even if it's just to breathe and relax for a bit. It means not running myself into the ground at full speed, 24/7.

"It's all good" instead of "It's all got to be perfect" has become more of my mantra lately, which feels amazing because it takes some of the pressure off of me to be "on" all the time.

Healthy living is working out in a way that I'm listening to my body. (Muscles too sore to hit the gym? Take today off! Bored with being stuck inside on a treadmill? Go for a surf or a hike instead.)

Healthy living is cooking meals for myself that I enjoy. Sitting down to read a book at night instead of watching TV. Putting down my phone after dinner and not looking at it again until morning. Shutting down my laptop at 5:00 p.m.

So it's become so much more than exercise. And extreme exercise seven days a week, for me anyway, is a thing of the past. Health has become more about self-care than about gym time, anyway. Sure, I love the gym because it makes me feel strong and is the perfect stress reliever, but it's not my entire life or my entire day. It's something I now do because I enjoy it, not because I feel like I have to do it.

I truly feel that I am the healthiest I've ever been at this very moment because now I am being honest with myself. Gentle with myself and with others. More balanced. I don't think I ever even knew what balance *was* because my daily life was to push myself back into a corner and worry about everyone else's needs before my own.

If that seems to be your pattern today, please: *Resist the urge.* In fact, I don't think I was able to grasp how bad my overall approach to healthy living had become…not until now. Until this moment when I don't have it anymore. And that "it" was always telling me to work harder, to do more, to never stop... in every aspect of my life. Being busy and running yourself into the ground to get everything accomplished isn't something to be proud of. It's an exhausting pattern that will follow you your entire life if you let it—not just during a breakup.

I'm not sure whether I thought something bad would happen if I told that voice in my head, the one that was always telling me to *go-go-go*, to shut the fuck up, but I never did.

The long and short of it, when it comes to your health, is this: If you don't take care of yourself mentally and physically, no one else will do it for you. You'll never be well-rounded. You will not be "okay." You will remain unbalanced, unhappy, and stuck in your own rut.

So get out, get up, slow down, and make yourself okay again. Own it.

There were other healthy habits that helped get my life back on track, and now I reflect on them, I realize how refreshingly simple they were. But simple and easy are two different things. If you're in the middle of a pain that is making you not only heartsick but bodily sick, here are few are simple-but-not-always-easy techniques that might help you heal.

Try to stop daily, even if it's just for ten minutes, and ask yourself, *Am I okay?* If the answer is no, then you must ask, *Why am I feeling like this?* In other words, learn to take your own inventory. Self-awareness became something I was really good at, and although I didn't always know how to fix it, I did know when I wasn't okay. During the worst of my pain, I'd honestly treat myself like a toddler, asking myself, *Kris, are you tired or hungry? If so, do not do anything or make any decision until you are no longer feeling one or both of these two things.*

Something else that was extremely important during the

time of my split was being able to give myself permission to sleep. To simply sleep! Whenever I felt tired, sad, depressed, or generally worn out (which was often), I'd usually be incredibly weepy and emotional, which was draining and exhausting.

Whenever I could, I'd just give myself permission to take a nap—whether it was 7:00 p.m. or noon! Granted, I'd rarely allow myself the luxury of spending the entire day in bed— I was aware *that* wasn't the healthy thing to do—but when I felt like I needed it, my bed was my refuge and a sound sleep was my friend.

Never be afraid of sleep. Unless, like anything, you begin doing it too much. Sleep heals. Sleep refreshes. Sleep soothes your soul and restores your body. Invite naps back into your life again. Treat yourself like a small child and keep the healing tactics simple (like naps and a snack).

There are other healthy ways to distract yourself from your own sadness that will bring back your balance and restore your emotional and physical health. But to benefit from them, to really avail yourself of the positive by-products that will result, you must put them into practice.

Here, I share a few practical quick-tips that will put you back on the road to healing and health. You'll also notice that you've seen a few of these tips mentioned before, in earlier chapters, which I actually count as a good thing because it points to the fact that a handful of simple suggestions can have a positive, across-the-board impact on your daily life on so many different levels. Hopefully they'll help you as much as they helped (and still help) me.

HEALTHY HABITS THAT WILL HELP YOU HEAL

WRITE! Toxic thoughts infecting your mind and body? Jotting them down might help get them out. Read them again the next day, the next week, or the next year to remind yourself of how far you've come.

FIND NEW FORMS OF FITNESS: Try a new fitness class each week, even if you suck at it. (I've done everything from Acro Yoga to 100-degree Pilates to crazy dance cardio. And let's just say, I'm not the best dancer in the world, but I loved at least giving it a shot.)

GET WITH YOUR GIRLFRIENDS: Refuse to isolate. Schedule workout dates with your girlfriends—so much more fun to me than a cocktail or a dinner date (and so much better for my abs!).

TEACH! If you're really into a certain workout regimen, get certified in it! Teaching others will help you. Healing people helps heal you.

DISCOVER HEALTHY NEW RECIPES: Scour the Internet for fun, healthy recipes. Come up with some recipes you haven't tried before. Then try them, even if you are cooking for one.

FOLLOW THE INSTRUCTORS: There's nothing wrong with finding the hottest fitness instructors in town and taking their classes just because you like to look at them—whatever gets you in the door.

RESEARCH WELLNESS RETREATS AND ACTUALLY GO ON ONE! Ask around. Search the Internet. Read up on the healthiest places to go...then go! It doesn't have to be an expensive, exotic locale. It can be as close as the day spa around the corner for a few hours of pampering. Just get up and get out.

SPRING FOR A NEW WORKOUT OUTFIT: Okay, so my collection of Spandex is overflowing and absolutely ridiculous, but it makes me feel good. How could I possibly be unhappy when I'm wearing pineapple print Spandex? Not possible.

*

Although I didn't realize it until I began writing this book, the process of helping others to heal is, well, contagious. It is happily contagious. It can begin with one person, then spread to another, and before you know it, one person's healing journey has become a collective project—a group journey toward health and wholeness.

Who knew, in the process of writing this book (and this chapter on health and healing in particular), that I'd be furthering my *own* continued healing?

It brings me right back to Rumi's quote. Right back to that essential truth about each and every one of us that binds us together into one collective whole. Even though the problems we face are our own, we don't need to feel so isolated and alone as we travel through them because someone else is also experiencing the same thing.

As you seek your own new healthy place, try to be a ladder for others. A light. A beacon. Because in helping others get back to health, you are helping yourself, too.

I know this because I am living it. Right at this very moment, as I am writing these words. Thank you for helping me continue to heal. And here, as I close, I must return to Rumi's words, not only because they spoke so eloquently to my heart yesterday but also because they will speak to your healing heart today.

*"Be a lamp, or a lifeboat or a ladder.
Help someone's soul heal."*

—Rumi

CHAPTER TEN

GRAB YOUR PASSPORT

"Not all those who wander are lost."

—J.R.R. Tolkien

During the Summer of the Split, in August, I planned a trip out to L.A., where I had a few very dear friends. These were people who knew me as Kris, not as Wife Kris or About-to-be-Ex-Wife Kris, or as Part-of-a-Couple Kris.

Just Kris.

I got to the airport feeling pretty apprehensive and not looking forward to the long flight across the country. I hadn't done any traveling since the split, and I was still in that uneasy stage of feeling like I was living this very surreal awful dream. When checking in, I decided to splurge and pay to change my shitty seat in the back of the plane to something closer to the front and more comfortable. Praying that whoever I was seated beside would just leave me alone (or wouldn't hate me because I had taken what was supposed to be an empty seat beside them).

When I got to my row, I looked down to a friendly face of a guy who looked to be about my age and suddenly I became pretty chatty. I'm pretty sure in a span of five minutes I had offered him snacks, told him about how I needed a change of scenery, and talked about how excited I was to get to L.A. I also offered him a ride to his friend's house where he was staying. Oh boy...

I couldn't tell if he was horrified he was now stuck beside a talkative human or happy to have a distraction for the five-hour flight, so I decided to cap the conversation off with, "Also, I just had a glass of tequila and will be asleep in ten minutes. Don't worry—you won't have to talk to me for much longer."

That conversation pretty much set the vibe for my entire L.A. trip—a good one (and I'm happy to report that, a few years later, Jon and I are still great friends—even if my tequila-driven chattiness had him thinking I was crazy for the first fifteen minutes of our friendship). It was filled with meeting new people, fun interactions, and a different way of thinking for me. I could be "just Kris" no matter what the future would hold for me. I could be whoever and whatever I wanted to be—I could be a new person.

That one short week away visiting my friends on the West Coast ended up being one of the most significant trips I'd ever take, for more than one reason. Yes, I desperately needed a respite from New York City and the Hamptons, but I returned to New York feeling so refreshed, so replenished, and so much more centered. I remember asking myself, *Why the hell can't I just move out there? What's holding me back?*

I'd been to L.A. many times before that, visiting friends and hanging out, but I still consider that singular August getaway as a powerful, pivotal experience and a defining moment in my larger life transition.

Why? Because being out there opened up the possibility of a new life—something I couldn't really fathom before I went. A different place. Fresh soil. Blue skies, sunshine, and comfortable comradery, rather than the dark, depressing, grey skyline and even darker emotional energy that threatened to swallow me up back in New York.

It didn't really take me too long after I got back to realize that it was indeed time to get the hell out of Dodge, even if just for a short period of time (at that point, I wasn't mentally ready to make a significant long-term move and life upheaval). My heart needed lifting. My mind needed clearing. Even my brain and my body needed a new momentum—a *positive* new momentum.

So, not too long thereafter, I did it. I took the plunge.

I packed up my suitcase and started to travel.

That's what one trip can do, especially when you're facing a crisis back home or you are in the middle of a swirl of negative energy. This is why getaways are good. They can open up your mind, clear both your vision *and* your head, and serve as a healthy reminder that there is, indeed, another way to live. Another place to be. Another journey to experience or possibly, even, a new life to live.

So, already in this chapter, I offer you a healthy reminder of how good a vacay—or even a staycay—can be for your body, mind, and spirit. It doesn't have to be permanent, and it doesn't have to exotic; all you need to do is put your feet on different soil for a little while. It's a wonderful, non-stressful way to jumpstart your journey on the road to recovery. *Try to do it.*

*

As I mentioned, that trip to L.A. was so good for me for so many reasons. By the time I returned to New York, I'd been bitten by the travel bug. Eaten up, in fact.

I'd returned feeling more comfortable and confident than I'd felt in a long, long time, with a bounce in my step and a lighter heart. I yearned for another getaway. To be somewhere other than I was. And here I should make myself clear: I don't consider travel to be running away from problems. I consider it a chance to escape for a little bit.

I listened to my heart again, and by that October I was in Italy. In Taormina, Sicily.

It was the first time I'd traveled out of the country solo, and although I was going to meet a group of people (all strangers) for a health retreat, I made a point to remind myself to do things by myself while I was there. I'm so glad I made that promise to myself *before* I left because it allowed me to focus more fully on accomplishing that goal while I was there, which brings me to another lesson I need to share: Never be afraid to fly solo, at any point in your life. These can be the most important journeys of all.

Even during the retreat, which was wonderful, I made it a point to get off by myself, alone. Single. Solitary. Comfortable in the depths of my own solitude. Being clear on what you want to accomplish on an upcoming trip is just as important a part of the journey. You owe it to yourself to plan carefully before you leave and to execute that plan once you arrive.

In fact, even before I left for Sicily, I jotted down a quick-list of all the things I *wouldn't* do while I was there.

1. No strict diets.

2. No working out in a gym.

3. No leading every conversation with the fact that I was

going through a divorce.

4. No social media. (Taking photos, yes; posting, no.)

I approached this trip with a real sense of purpose and intention, and I'm glad I did it this way. It served me well. I also made a list of the things I *would* do.

1. Write a lot.

2. Eat a lot of incredible food.

3. Meet new people.

4. Get off by myself and fly solo whenever possible.

5. Be fully present for all of it.

Sicily is a stunning place, and I was staying in what I can only describe as a mansion surrounded by lush greenery. There was lots of land covered in vineyards, a beautiful pool, and healthy farm-to-table feasts laid out for every meal—a health retreat in every sense of the word.

I'd take day trips by myself and wander into the local bakeries in town, whose shelves were always filled with incredible homemade desserts. And I'm here to tell you I tried every single one of them. No calorie-counting allowed.

I went in search of the best pizza in Taormina and ate an entire pie by myself. I took myself out to dinners—long, sumptuous dinners with multiple courses and lots of wine. I'd basically given myself permission to *just be*—something I'd never "allowed" myself to do before. I would not overthink or over-plan this trip; I just did what I wanted when I wanted.

Again, I returned to New York feeling lighter. More centered. More directly (and deeply) connected to the larger world around me. I somehow felt less isolated.

My healing journey had begun.

Well, the travel bug continued to eat me up, and I happily surrendered. I was hopelessly, happily hooked, and after returning from Italy, I immediately began planning my next adventure.

A few months later, in December, at the height of the holiday season, I was off again. Destination: Tortola, in the British Virgin Islands, for a surf trip.

As I've mentioned before, the ocean is my happy place, and, fuck, my heart really needed happy at that point. Christmas in New York was a rough time for me; my first holiday season solo. Tortola was the perfect place for me to slip away to—an excellent escape.

I felt like I'd found Nirvana.

In Tortola, mornings meant pure joy. Fresh papaya and coffee for breakfast, followed by frolicking (there's really no other word for it) in the ocean. Afternoons were about as perfect as any afternoon could get. Surfing above the coral reef, bobbing happily in the bright blue, sparkling water. And every evening, witnessing the miracle of the most extraordinary sunsets I've ever seen. The sun was a giant fireball as bright orange, purple, and violet streaks marked the sky.

Yet even with all of that breathtaking beauty, anxiety still crept in. The feeling of being a bit lost and a little off-balance still squeezed in and tried to take up room in my heart and my mind.

So, I guess my other lesson is this: Even if you do take a healing journey to another place—whether it's to Maui or the local day spa—anxiety will follow you if you let it.

The trick here is to train yourself to seek tranquility from the *inside out*—not just from the outside in. Whether that's through writing, meditating, or reading—however you de-stress.

That way, you can take it with you wherever you go. No matter what you're facing or what part of the world you happen to be standing in.

Take it with you.

I was on a mission that December. I flew to Costa Rica directly from Tortola. But the anxiety continued to creep back in, trying its damnedest to get the best of me. My mood changed and darkness began to settle into my head, almost like a pounding headache that just wouldn't go away.

The flight there was awful. I was exhausted and my mind wasn't thinking right. I remember saying to myself, *What the hell am I doing? Where the hell am I going? Why don't I just fly home to Virginia so I won't be alone at Christmas?*

By the time I landed in Costa Rica on Christmas Eve, I was in a serious fuck-it mode. I was ready to cancel the whole trip. I wasn't sure I could survive staying there even a few days without breaking down, and my trip was supposed to last for two weeks. I'd reached my boiling point. All the tranquility I felt in Tortola had vanished, like smoke in the wind.

I'd arranged for a driver to pick me up at the airport for the two-hour drive to the resort (Well, *resort* is a grand word. How about *very inexpensive rustic jungle retreat?*). Within thirty minutes of the drive, I'd convinced him to stop for coconuts and watermelon sold on the side of the road, and he'd convinced me to play all of the newest pop hits on my iPhone (at full blast) since his van didn't have a radio.

How quickly things change. What a wonderful reminder that we are, indeed, in control of our mood and our temperament. I don't remember the exact point I pushed my own anxiety to the back seat, and eventually over the side of the cliff, but I do remember it got up and left...and it left during that drive from the airport.

I'll never forget that drive, that moment of freedom and returning tranquility. As I was drinking my fresh coconut, with my bare feet hanging out the window, barreling down a dirt road while singing as loudly as possible to teeny-bopper music with a man who had been a stranger a mere hour earlier, I remember thinking to myself, *You know what, Kris? You're going to be okay...*

I wrote about the trip, this life-defining trip, in my blog. Here's an excerpt of the post:

I read a quote by author Cheryl Strayed on the flight to Costa Rica that simply said, "How wild it was, to let it be." Let it be? What was "it" exactly? The constant nagging voice in my head, the questions about the future and what it held for me, job worries, family stuff? The list could go on really, but what if, what if I could just let it rest. Be wild, free.

Could I really do that?

The answer is yes, because that's what I did in Costa Rica. I threw my makeup bag in the bottom of my suitcase—never to be touched while I was there. I didn't wear shoes. I was coated in a thick layer of dust 24/7 as a mountain bike was my mode of transportation. Showers were taken in the ocean. Food was snagged at a local farmer's market—to be eaten with bare hands and knives on the beach. It tasted better that way. The simplicity of it was so freeing, so raw, so amazing.

Raw, that's the word...raw and fearless. There were no timelines, no schedules, no getting up to rush and go.

I understand that not everyone can up and fly off to Costa Rica, but we can all take a minute to look deep into ourselves and quiet the noise. Be honest about what it would mean to cleanse ourselves. Maybe that's just letting go of a friend who isn't good for you, breaking a bad habit, starting a new routine.

Am I making any sense? If not, I'm sorry…it's the jungle magic; it's still got me under its spell…

*

I returned from Costa Rica a new person—a calmer, more relaxed person who wasn't so scared of what the future might hold for her. But a trip to Cabo helped heal my hurting heart, too. This one wasn't solo, so the energy was completely different. A good girlfriend nudged me to go. Oh, that Ashley… she is truly the best.

Before my split, she'd invited me to her bachelorette party in Cabo, along with about twenty other girls. I'd politely declined; my marriage was crumbling, my heart was breaking, and I couldn't even think about going on a wild-and-free bachelorette party trip.

But as the trip grew closer, I began to change my mind, and I said to Ashley, "You know, I'm sure you don't have room on your trip anymore, but I really should have booked my spot to go with you guys."

What she said next is one of the many, many reasons I love her so: "Oh, that's great, because I'd already saved a spot for you on the trip from the very start. I just had a feeling you would need it."

So she'd known that I needed the getaway even before I knew it. And she was kind enough, present enough as the good friend that she is, to take the necessary steps to make it happen.

That trip involved lots of laughs, lots of tequila, and lots of running around in my bikini, but I felt wild and free again, which was precisely what I needed at the time.

When it comes to getting away, though, remember this: Not every trip has to have such dramatic impact, some huge lesson to learn. These trips can just be fun—a distraction and nothing more, and that's okay, too. Also, not every journey must end in some exotic, expensive locale. The important thing is to get up, get moving, and get out.

It can be a solo day trip somewhere local, like a sizzling journey to a beautiful white sand beach, or just a simple staycation with a good girlfriend. The point is that you place yourself in different space than the one you're currently in. Get away.

Get the hell away.

*

Travel can also be to the benefit of others, another way to heal. At least it was for me during one special trip.

I coordinated a women's wellness retreat in Costa Rica (my second time there) that turned my life around. Signing up thirteen other women to join me in the middle of the Costa Rican jungle for what I considered to be a healing retreat—most of them never having met each other before—was more than a notion.

I arrived a few days early in order to prep the menu and coordinate the fitness program and itinerary. I wanted these women, most of them stressed, overscheduled, and under-appreciated, *to take time out for themselves.* This was something I had never been good at, and I wanted to help others get to this place of self-love.

I wanted them to reconnect with nature and know what it felt like to be wild and free—precisely what I had gained from that first trip to Costa Rica. I wanted to help these women heal from whatever they might be going through—minor things, big things, or just daily life that was stressful. This was my dream for them.

During that trip, we *all* grew. We *all* discovered new strength that we never even knew we had. Friendships were forged. Trust was established and challenges were overcome.

Here they were trusting *me* to take care of them in another country (in the middle of the jungle, no less) and just as hard (or even harder) was that they were trusting themselves to make new friends. The age range was from about twenty-one to fifty, and it was so incredible to see them putting themselves out there like that. To this day, some of the women have remained friends, and they hail from all over the globe. New York City. Boston. Canada. England. Singapore.

Witnessing their personal transformation during this time was amazing. A lot of the women who had children and husbands back at home were obviously unaccustomed to putting themselves first. But after about a day or two, these women were surfing. Singing. Running barefoot and dirty through the jungle. Reading in hammocks. Hiking along the beach. They surrendered to their "wild" side and as each day passed, I could see the change in them. The growth. It was incredible.

And as I witnessed their unfolding, I felt my own spirit unfolding, too. In helping others, I was helping myself heal, too.

*

I can't emphasize enough the importance of taking a solo trip. You'll absorb wisdom you never expected and learn life lessons you didn't see coming. You'll learn how to be alone— and hopefully will learn to love it. Even if it's not something you're accustomed to (and for most women it isn't because we're conditioned to believe that we must be attached to someone else when traveling, particularly abroad), try to make it a priority to break away, break free, and get by yourself, even if it's just for a little while.

You need to hear your own voice. Sit within your own space.

I remember on one of the last nights in Taormina, I took myself out to dinner to a place recommended to me by a local I'd met during my stay. As soon as I sat, the waiter came over and said to me, "Bella, bella. Are you not waiting for someone?"

My solo dining experience seemed to confuse him.

"Isn't someone *meeting* you?" he asked again, confounded.

I looked up at him and answered confidently, "No, signore, it's just me."

It's just me.

I am enough.

There I sat, having this incredibly sumptuous meal by myself. Cherishing every bite.

I was alone, but I was not lonely.

And you know what? I also ordered *four* desserts that night and ate all four of them. By myself.

How's that for empowering?

*

Here are some simple getaway suggestions for when you need to break free, and these are ideas that can become a reality on *any* budget:

TRAVEL TIPS FROM KRIS

- Visit a friend who lives in a different city or state. It's a free place to stay, a change of scenery, and a great chance to get away with a good girlfriend.

- Swap homes/apartments for the weekend with someone you know.

- Book yourself a blow-out, dress yourself up, and take yourself out for a nice dinner afterward. Fly solo.

- Invite a friend to come visit you for the weekend and act like a tourist in your own town. See the sights through fresh eyes.

- Make a list of all the places you've always wanted to travel to, then set the goal of saving up and going on at least one trip within the year. It's always good to have something to look forward to.

Getaways don't have to be complicated either. My girlfriend Jocelyn and I spent a few months during the winter doing our own staycation weekends, and they were wonderful. We'd spend the weekend going to different workouts, finding organic grocery stores, trying out new recipes (cooking ourselves these massive healthy dinners), and reading.

It was our cost-effective version of getting away, and I looked forward to those weekends so much. They were easy, fun, and provided the comfortable, hassle-free companionship we both needed without the pressure of going out, dressing up, looking good, or talking to strangers. (Joc and I had been friends since college, so this was a really old school, tried-and-true, comfortable friendship.)

The options are limitless. But you must be fearless, bold, and imaginative as you go about planning your getaways.

Do it soon.

Do it for yourself, because as I always say, nobody else is going to do it for you.

Happy travels! Wherever they might lead you.

"Travel brings power and love back into your life."

—Rumi

CHAPTER ELEVEN

WHEN FAILURE HELPS YOU SUCCEED

"Failure is success if we learn from it."

—Malcom Forbes

*W*hen it comes to failure, I'm just going to be honest: It takes a lot of guts to figure out why you fucked up. Even more to accept the fact that fucking up, failing miserably, falling flat on your ass every now and then, all of these things will actually *help* you in the long run.

All of these things will help you grow.

It took me a long time—most of my life—to realize that if things are always going right in your life (or seeming to go right), you're never really learning anything because you're too busy playing it safe. Living too carefully. Clinging to the edge of the pool rather than pushing out into the deep water where life can get dangerous and scary and, yes, pretty fucked up on occasion.

Sinking—even drowning sometimes, as long as you can eventually revive yourself—does have its advantages. Value and meaning can be found in messing up, as long as you treat the experience as a life lesson and dig deep to find out not only what went wrong but what you did to *make* it go wrong.

Ownership is involved.

This is something I didn't truly acknowledge until my divorce. I would jump from failure to failure (not only in relationships but in life in general) without taking the time to figure out why what I had done had failed. I'd push forward at breakneck speed without asking, *Where did I go wrong and what was my part in all of this?*

It's so much easier to blame failure on others. To run from your mistakes. To ignore your issues. To be a victim and make excuses. To stay stuck in those vicious cycles of resentment, rage, and admittedly, sometimes even revenge. This is when you make the mistake of allowing your failure to get the best of you. This is when you allow your failure to push you underwater and hold you there, kicking and screaming, until you drown.

Instead of fighting failure, though, *embrace* it. Use it like the tool that it is. Treat it like a life preserver that will keep you afloat rather than an anchor that will drag you under.

Don't misunderstand me. I enjoy a smooth-sailing ride as much as the next person, but when I *do* sink, when I *do* get swallowed up by that monster wave, I've now learned to let it take me under—for a minute—before I push my way back up and figure out where the hell I went wrong.

This is not only how I learned to surf but how I eventually learned to *live*, and I'm healthy, happy, whole, and alive today because of it (not to mention a pretty kick-ass surfer. I mean, yes, I fall and I fail…but it's *fun*).

After my divorce, I realized that all the excuses I made for myself weren't going to work anymore because I wasn't being honest with myself about my issues. Something had to give. If I didn't bring myself to a place of raw honesty and total truth, I was going to keep on making the same mistakes for the rest of my life. I was going to keep perpetuating the same tired old toxic patterns. I was going to continue fucking up and not learning from it.

Honesty became a must. If I wasn't honest about what I'd done to fail in my marriage, I probably wasn't going to be honest about anything else in my life, either.

I needed to turn that tide. I actually wrote out a list of things I believed I had done wrong. Let me tell you, seeing an actual list of shitty things about yourself will either sink you further or give you the ass-kicking you need to do better, to be better.

After embracing that realization, I felt more empowered. More in control. After a divorce, a bad breakup, or even a difficult-but-necessary separation from a good friend, it's pretty empowering to look in a mirror and honestly say, *You know what? You fucked up.* Or, *You fucked up at least half of your relationship. Now what are you going to do about it?*

And here—speaking of ownership—I'm going to own up to something I've never said or even written before: *My biggest regret from my failed marriage was that I wasn't open and honest with how I was feeling 100 percent of the time (or most of the time, really). I was a terrible communicator. I wasn't honest with myself, with my ex, or with the people who loved me and were genuinely concerned about my happiness (or lack thereof).*

I was too busy people-pleasing, too busy making sure everybody else was satisfied, too busy desperately trying to paint that ever-present portrait of perfection to worry myself about honesty. Self-honesty, that is. This was one of the heaviest anchors that took me down.

I'm not saying that my being honest and openly communicative would have saved our relationship, but it would have helped at the end, when I just shut down completely because I had so many raw and angry feelings eating me from the inside out.

If I'd only been more forthright at the end of it all, instead of keeping everything bottled up inside, at least my anguish would not have been so deep. Complete and total openness would have lightened the entire load.

As usual, though—and, here, the mindful mantra that hopefully flows throughout this book—I've learned from my faults. I've grown from my grief. I've become stronger (and wiser) because of my failures. I have taken the mistakes I made back then and turned them into life lessons and daily practices that I still live by today, right now, at this very moment.

Through hard work, raw honesty, and deliberate attempts on my part to push myself toward growth, I have allowed my failures to work for me.

Today, I speak my mind (but not in an aggressive way). Today, I only have people in my life who respect me. I value my self-worth. I value my opinion enough to want to express it openly and without hesitation. Most important, I'm honest with myself about what I'm feeling…even if I am wrong. I don't have to be right all the time.

I think that's a mistake we all make. Being honest about how you are feeling in the moment doesn't have to mean that you are right. It can simply mean it's just how you feel. And it's okay to be wrong.

Today I am honest, and I feel a constant, compelling need to be respected.

*

Not until now have I really given any deep and serious thought to where my feelings about failure actually originated. Why was I so afraid to fail in the beginning?

Not until now did I realize I've been carrying the answer—and the origin—within me all along. This requires a look back.

Way, way back, to the very beginning.

As a little girl (and I mention this in the beginning of the book), I was the quiet one, the one who played it safe. I could typically be found reading a book, playing quietly in my room—you know, following the rules, keeping everyone satisfied, and trying not to make any waves. (Who knew that I'd one day evolve into a woman who loved riding those waves, not only on a surfboard in the middle of the ocean, but in the way I live my daily life?) Rocking the boat was something I never wanted to do.

I avoided failure—or even the *possibility* of failure—at all costs. Hell, if something scared me, I would just stop doing it.

I remember once I fell off my bike when I was in fifth grade and busted both of my front teeth. Even now, thinking back on it, I can still feel the horror of it all—not just the horror and pain of falling down and sustaining an injury, but even worse, the horror and pain of being called "Fang" and other mean-spirited names by the other kids at school.

Let me tell you: I never wanted to get back on my bike again.

I'd fallen. I'd failed. I'd wiped out, in more ways than one. And rather than facing my fears (like getting back on my bike and taking back control) or learning from my mistakes (reminding myself to never, ever ride over wet leaves or wide cracks in the sidewalk again), I simply retreated inside of myself—the most dangerous place to be right after a crisis occurs.

After that, I never wanted to fail again. I never wanted to *fall* again, literally or figuratively. In my mind, failure was bad.

A sign of weakness. I didn't know then what I know today: Falling is not a sign of weakness but a sign of strength. That it is necessary—even mandatory—for growth and change.

It wasn't just my bruising bicycle experience, though; it was a million other encounters, large and small, during my childhood that helped mold and form my feelings about failure. That's how we form our personalities and our perspective, by basing it on prior experience.

So my fear of failure, I now recognize, followed me from childhood into early adulthood, and that fear helped contribute, later in my life, to failed relationships and unhealthy alliances.

But my early life wasn't *all* about fear and failure. It was about finding joy and strength, too. And it was the beauty of this balance that helped bring me to the place I am today...that, and a hell of a lot of hard work on my part.

Looking back now—with more acute vision—I *do* remember watching my parents take chances. My dad never played it safe in his career, for example. He was a farmer who decided to move into the corporate world, who went to law school (with three school-aged kids at home), and who then returned to farming.

My mom, too, was confident and unafraid. Even when she was raising the three of us, she always worked and was constantly supportive of my father's efforts and, yes, sometimes his crazy ideas. And she always, always believed in her kids. Maybe most important, I now realize, she always believed in *herself.*

In fact, when she found out I was writing this book, she made it her business to go back and look through my baby book for a favorite quote that she'd given me long ago. I'm not sure who actually said these words, but I do know that they have as much meaning today as they did decades ago when my mother first pasted them into my photo album:

"There's a part of me that wants to make life perfect for my daughter, but I know I can't protect her. I need to allow her to go out and experience pain and sickness. Being a mother is not magical; it isn't always easy to recognize her right to live her own life."

Those words and that strength are something, I now realize, that I never really thanked my mother for. I probably should have because witnessing those traits in her with my own eyes was, for me, life-defining and maybe even life-saving.

So here, I must give gratitude where it is due. For it is long, long overdue:

Thank you, MommaCakes, for raising us right and for teaching us, through your own actions, that failure isn't a sign of weakness but a sign of strength, as long as we learn from our mistakes. Thank you for teaching me that important lesson, even though I didn't fully absorb its wisdom until, well, now.

So, yes, I watched both my parents take chances in their own lives, and now I recognize that the more I watched them, the more it actually helped me. The more it solidified within me—deep down—that falling is okay and right and necessary, as long as you force yourself to get back up again. It's a piece of wisdom I embrace today, but it literally took me a lifetime to learn.

*

Failure isn't exclusive to just romantic relationships, either. Friendships can buckle, wobble, and finally give out, too. I've created a term for failed friendships—and it springs from the failures I've had in the past. I call it the Broken Bird Syndrome.

Before I went through my big breakup, I had lots of friends who needed to be "fixed." These were people experiencing strife and strain in their own lives and needed (or at least I thought they needed) my kind and nurturing attention. They were like little broken birds who needed to be coddled before they could be set free again, before they could be lifted to the lowest branch and encouraged to fly again.

This in and of itself set me up for failure in a lot of my friendships because it's such a one-sided thing. I'd spend my time fixing friends, doting on people and their problems, people (I realized later) who didn't really care all that much about *me.* They were just happy to take, take, take. And to be completely honest, many of them had pretty major, messy issues that I simply couldn't see because I was too busy taking care of them.

What I have learned from this Broken Bird Syndrome, from these failures—and what you can learn, too, if you take this wisdom to heart and apply it in your life—is that friendship has to be a two-way street. Each person must care about the other *equally.* A true and lasting friendship can't be one-sided. Balance is mandatory. A one-sided friendship is doomed to fail. Just like a one-sided romantic relationship is bound to fail, too.

Perhaps a clarification is needed here concerning failed relationships: I don't really think *any* relationship ending is a failure as long as you learn something from it. That it ended is not a failure, really, but a necessary transition to its next stage.

I guess what I'm trying to say is that sure, relationships can *end*, but coming to an end doesn't have to mean it failed. It just redefined itself. Split off in a different direction. If it has to end for any reason, that's not a failure to me; it's just that it didn't work out.

You learn. You grow. You move on. And hopefully, you move on to something that is better, brighter, and more positive. Some failures (and I truly believe this) can just be fuck-ups. And that's okay, too. Maybe the only thing you learn from the relationship is that it shouldn't have happened. Or that whatever mistakes you did make, you will not make again in the future.

Whatever happens in your relationships—bad or good, negative or positive—you have to try to learn from it.

Because *not* learning from your missteps is the greatest tragedy of all.

"I know this transformation is painful, but you're not falling apart; you're falling into something different, with a new capacity to be beautiful."

—William C. Hannan

CHAPTER TWELVE

DATE ALL OF THE WRONG PEOPLE

Bumble.

Raya.

The League.

Tinder.

*T*his is what I was presented with when I started dating again after my split. My initial thought was, *What the fuck* (swipe…swipe)–the second thought was, *You've got to be kidding me.*

If all of these words I listed at the beginning don't ring a bell, don't feel left out of the loop (even though you kind of are). I didn't know them, either. But these words represent the new language of love.

Or at least lust. Or…hookups.

Who knew that dating apps, profile pics, and a left-to-right swipe would one day become the hottest way to meet people?

Not me, that's for sure. But this was the world I stepped into right after my split.

Damn.

I've mentioned before that one of my habits in the past

was to jump from one committed relationship to another. (A mistake, I know, but that's just the way it was.)

For this reason alone, I never really had the time, the desire, or the opportunity for casual dating. I was always involved in a relationship. Always attached (stuck might be the better word) to someone's side, comfortable only when I was clinging to or fixing someone. I never *not* wanted to be the smallest part of a larger whole. I look back now and see myself as a different Kris. I was stuck like glue to the person beside me, worried more about my partner than about myself.

Getting adjusted to life in the single lane was no easy task. Granted, the dating world had changed dramatically, but as you might imagine, I wasn't *about* to let it pass me by. So I tried to jump in. Maybe not with both feet, but I was going to prove to the world that I was fine—more than fine—and could easily adjust to this different dating world. (You know, the Super Woman perfectionist thing again.)

I'll admit it: In the year after my split, I did check out a few of those dating apps. I created a couple of profiles and swiped a few photos. But I soon discovered that world wasn't really for me. It felt too fake. Too robotic. It was such an odd game, one that I wasn't really interested in playing. In fact, I didn't actually go out on a single date from an app.

And you know me by now: I don't do well with fake. I need real. I was looking for genuine interactions with real humans. I wanted face to face, not some Internet dating scheme.

That's not to say I didn't go on a lot of casual dates the year after my split. I did, but I met these people in real life situations. I also knew that none of the guys I went out with during that time was going to end up meaning that much to me in the long run.

Were they fun to get to know? Some of them, sure. Was it

fun to go out for an occasional dinner? Of course it was. But I learned very early on not to treat those casual dates as a serious, substantive part of my future. These weren't people I was going to end up with for the long haul; they just gave me a reason to get out and be social. To see new faces. Try something different.

And now I think about it, what the hell is so wrong with that?

Casual dating does, in fact, have its place. If nothing else, it can open your eyes to what you *don't* want in a relationship. It facilitates the weeding-out process and gets you out of the house at the same time.

Plus, I didn't really know who I was after the split. How could I possibly find the time and the energy to get to know someone else on a serious level when I didn't even really know myself? How could I meet an amazing long-term partner if I wasn't whole yet? It just wouldn't have been fair (or realistic) to look at the guys I was going out with at that time as potential for the future.

I wasn't in the right headspace for all of that.

So, if you're just coming out of a marriage or a long-term relationship and thinking about easing back into the wonderful/ awful world of casual dating, go into it with an open mind and try to manage your own expectations. What do you want to get out of the date? An evening of fun or an eventual wedding proposal? (Note: Go into NO DATE thinking of weddings, EVER!) My suggestion is to simply start at the beginning and with low expectations, which is always the best place to be. Go into it with the desire to have fun, that's all.

Nothing's wrong with a nice dinner out with someone you've just met, but it's rarely realistic (or desirable, even) to start picking out the engagement ring the week after your first date.

What I realized during the year after my split is that too

many women seem to date with a purpose, an end goal, in mind. There's always got to be this *tangible takeaway*. And what's the takeaway? What's the ultimate goal? What do we tell ourselves after each and every date? That marriage is the reason we're jumping through these hoops in the first place; marriage is the final destination.

That's a mistake.

Dating doesn't always have to lead to marriage. And marriage doesn't always have to be the end-all-be-all of a relationship.

All I'm saying is that dates don't always have to equal serious relationships, sex doesn't always have to equal love, and love doesn't always have to be manufactured, manipulated, or forced into becoming matrimony.

If you've decided to put yourself back out there on the dating scene, try not to be disappointed if all the dinners don't eventually lead to that trip down the aisle.

This *gotta-get-married* mentality—the constant strategizing and, frankly, the desperate thinking—gives lots of women a bad rap, and it undercuts the potential for plain old commitment-free fun. Try not to let a casual crush or a shared meal turn into the Desperate Search to Find a Husband. Just let a dinner be a dinner. Don't always have an end-game in mind.

Just let it be a damn dinner.

*

By now, you know that I'm a big believer in learning from your mistakes. Some of the most valuable lessons (at least in my life, anyway) have come from the middle of my darkest moments and from the depths of my dumbest mistakes. In fact, I can't think of a time where I *didn't* learn something valuable from a misstep, which doesn't make it a misstep at all but a life lesson.

Dating is the same way.

I was only half-joking when I titled this chapter because I really do believe that there's value to be found in dating a few completely-wrong-for-you people along the way.

Why? Because like I said earlier, it opens up your eyes to how you *don't* want to be treated in future relationships. It helps you set your bar. In fact, dating a...well, dating a *dick*... can actually be really *empowering*.

I speak from experience. And let me tell you this: Dating an absolute asshole (or just a wrong-for-you human) forces you into absolute action—and if it doesn't, it sure as hell should. The formula is simple enough. If you don't like him, even if you think you should, if he's completely wrong for you, or if he's turning out to be a real jerk, just walk away.

Walk away.

Why drag things out?

In the year after my split, I went on my fair share of bad dates. But here's my lemon-to-lemonade rationale: Instead of being discouraged or depressed, I learned some lessons, weeded out the jerks, and gave myself permission to keep on stepping. I didn't allow myself to stay stuck. So dating a real dick can have very real advantages. It can really give you the momentum you need to move right along.

Most times in life, bad can be good.

My mantra all over again.

*

Any chapter on dating has *got* to include at least a little bit of dishing—and though dishing isn't usually my style, here I just can't resist. So I'm going to share a few eye-opening "dating" encounters. Because everyone has to have a few of those.

It's funny, actually, how these scenes still bounce around

in my memory, even though they happened years ago. And it was actually fun recalling them and writing them down for this book. (As opposed to looking back on them like, *What was I thinking?* It was refreshing to laugh about them.)

I was standing in a coffee shop wearing pineapple-print Spandex (as one does on a Saturday morning) when I first met Guy #1.

I was newly single then, still pretty fresh out of my marriage. Looking back, I realize it was probably a little too early to start dating, but I did it anyway. Being the headstrong woman that I am, I wanted to move full-speed ahead. Wanted to send the impression to the world that I was okay. In full control. Ready for anything.

But back to the coffee shop. Back to the Spandex.

I placed my coffee order, stepped aside, then promptly bumped into a tall, handsome man who'd deemed it necessary to wear a trucker hat and aviator sunglasses at 8:00 in the morning. Um, okay, guy. Calm it down…

I looked up at him (it was a stretch because he was 6'4") and said something like, "That's really a look you've got going on… aviators and a huge hat are kind of overkill, no?"

Guy #1 looked down at me and said, "The girl wearing pineapple Spandex is really going to comment on my choice of morning attire?"

"Well-played, sir. Well played," I answered back…and just like that, the flirting had begun.

It wasn't until he took off his sunglasses that I realized I'd been harassing a very well-known actor—pre-caffeine, no less.

Whoops.

We began talking, and before I knew it he'd asked for my number. Then he walked out, and I went on with my day. Um… what just happened here? I remember thinking to myself.

We ended up going to dinner that night, sitting outside and talking until 4:00 a.m. We saw each other the next day as well, spending the entire time talking on the beach, until he had to drive back to the city to film his latest movie. He was insanely funny, as most comedic actors are, plus he was charming and handsome.

I was pretty enamored…that is, until I didn't see him (except for a lot of texts, which in my mind does not count as an actual interaction) for three months. But when he texted to say that he was back in NYC and to ask if I'd like to go to dinner, well, I jumped at the offer. (Dummy.)

We went out to a really nice but very public place (people staring, paparazzi avoiding, the whole deal). Afterwards, yet again, we sat and talked until 4:00 a.m. For some reason, he felt comfortable enough to confide in me some pretty deep, dark stuff. If I'd been a shitty person, I would have sold those stories to the tabloids. (But I'm not, so I didn't.)

Guy #1 spoke about how hard his divorce was, and I think we were really able to bond about that—we were just two broken human beings trying to find our way, both exiting relationships that were not meant for us.

Are you waiting for the lesson here? Waiting for that lightning bolt from the sky to strike and spread wisdom all over the place? It's coming …

So Guy #1 went off again to film another movie. Again, besides the texts, I didn't see him again until we went hiking together in L.A. (At that point I'd just been living there for a week.)

Yet again, we spent hours together as he poured his heart out about the things that were going on in his life, and I was pretty sure he hadn't shared this stuff with anyone else because it would have for sure ended up in a tabloid.

It was on that hiking date I realized that, as much as I liked

Guy #1, I was just being the easy one. Always available. Always ready to lend a listening ear. I was easy to talk to, easy to be around, never challenging him on his disappearing acts. Hell, easily fitting into his schedule whenever he wanted to see me.

The next time he came back around (via text) to ask me out to dinner—on his schedule, of course—I said quite simply, "No thanks."

I wasn't mean. I wasn't angry. I was just not going to be the girl he called anytime he needed a therapist to have dinner with. I've got more self-respect for myself than that. To my surprise, after I explained how I felt, he said I was completely right and apologized profusely. Boy, did it feel damn good to walk away from that one. Even if he was charming, funny, and good-looking. Even if I had to constantly see his face on billboard when his new show came out. Sigh.

Damn good.

*

My point is this: If someone—anyone!—is not making time for you, or if they're fitting you into their schedule only when it's convenient for them and playing the disappearing act while still keeping you on hook via text, and all they talk about is themselves, the relationship is not a two-way street. Even if they're a hot celebrity with multiple movies coming out and a huge TV career—*stop seeing them.*

A selfish human being is a selfish human being, no matter how large the bank account or how many movie screens their face appears on. It also doesn't make them a bad person; they just have different priorities than you do.

Learn to demand that others treat you with the same high level of respect that you treat yourself—and don't settle for anything less.

Learn from your mistakes, refuse to settle, and if you feel like you're being used or manipulated, just walk away. No drama, no anger, just walk.

It's that simple.

*

Another of my celebrity encounters turned out to be equally eye-opening and equally frustrating. I'll call him Guy #2.

Guy #2 started off much the same way as Guy #1. He was another well-known actor—I should have learned after round one of actor dating—and when we first met, he was charming and very attentive. Calling (I mean, who calls anymore?), texting, dinners multiple nights in a row, hanging out at his beach house to avoid paparazzi. The whole bit.

In the short time we were seeing each other, we spent a lot of time together. He'd confide in me be about his fears of reporters writing nasty articles about him and his fear of facing upcoming auditions. He told me about his family and how close he was to his mom. He was always very pleasant with me (although, again, didn't seem to care too much about what I had going on in my life), but he had a reputation for not being a very nice guy...a side of him I didn't see at first.

It was only after I'd purchased and delivered a nice dinner to his apartment (because he was hungry and didn't want to leave) and he offered to call me an Uber instead of wanting to hang out with me that I realized, um, this guy is kind of rude and self-centered and probably gives zero shits about me and my well-being. His initial attention-giving personality was just an act to get me hooked.

When I told him I wasn't interested in seeing him anymore, I'm not sure he actually believed me (I'm also not sure he was that sad about it, either...) because who in the hell would turn down a well-known actor? It was only after six weeks of not seeing him anymore that I think he got it. Maybe...

"Hey, are you free?" he texted me one night when he tried to reach me. "If so, hop a flight to NYC right now. Tonight. We're going to Italy."

Um, what the fuck? *I'm thinking.*

I'd finally had enough, and finally, finally realized I'd been allowing him to treat me like, well, kind of like shit. I'd gone beyond my saturation point—which is sometimes exactly where we need to be in order to push ourselves into action.

I took action, all right.

"Thanks for the offer," I said, sweet as sugar. And what I said next even surprised me, it came from so out of the blue, "But I've met someone. A guy that I've been friends with who is amazing and kind and not at all self-absorbed. So I guess I'll be turning down your trip because I'm hoping he likes me, too." I never got a response to that text or heard from him again for that matter. Good riddance.

The point is that no matter *who* the guy is, or what the guy does, or how much money said guy pulls down every month or every week (or every movie), if he's not respecting you, *ditch his ass.* If he's not nice to you or just plain old disrespectful, I'll say it again: *Ditch his ass.*

And don't be sad about it! Or annoyed, for that matter. It's not worth the wasted energy.

*

So the lessons, when it comes to casual dating, are these: If you're going to have a fun, casual date, have a fucking fun, casual date. Don't make it into matrimony, and don't get yourself all hung-up. If he treats you like shit, walk away. If it turns negative, make lemons out of lemonade and use it as a learning experience. Don't even get mad about it; simply manage your expectations and just stop seeing someone if they aren't good for you.

If it works, great. If it doesn't, chalk it up to experience and keep on moving. Have a good time with it. Share a few laughs. Eat a good meal. And through it all, remember this:

It's just a damn dinner.

"The best kind of lovers are the ones who arrive without a proper invitation."

—R.M. Drake

CHAPTER THIRTEEN

NEW LIFE, NEW DIRECTION

*"Your life does not get better by chance.
It gets better by change."*

—Jim Rohn

*N*ew York City is a tough place to live even when you're *happy*; it's almost unbearable when you're sad. At least it was for me. The fast pace and the harsh people, the concrete and the cold weather, all of it felt like it was starting to stack up against me. (*Bury* me is the better description.)

It also carried with it too many memories of my old life.

I remember the moment I came to the conclusion that I needed to move. I remember, even then, how arriving at this conclusion felt like an important pivotal point in my life. It hit me like a ton of bricks.

In order to survive this, I have to make a change.

Moving to L.A. would be an easy transition. I had amazing

friends in California. I was familiar with the city from traveling there so often, and I was pretty sure that the combination of palm trees + sunshine would = happy.

Or at least less sad.

I needed to change my environment to clear my head. What I *needed*, when it came right down to it, was a healthy, sunny, wide-open space where I could sort my shit out. A place that carried fewer memories of my past.

I'm not saying that moving made me instantly, totally happy, but it did put me on a better path to being okay. Sure, I had my share of freak-out moments just after I arrived—*Did I make the right decision? Should I have moved so quickly? What the hell was I thinking?*—but those moments came less and less frequently as my fears began to fade and I began to find my new rhythm.

I'm just glad/relieved/proud/happy that I actually *listened* to my inner voice when it told me to make a change and save my own life.

This is true for anyone going through a breakup or simply going through the eye of their own personal storm: Being able to listen to your inner voice, heed your silent instinct, yield to that deep-in-the-pit-of-your-stomach intuition will be what keeps you okay. What keeps you sane.

Maybe even what keeps you alive.

I know. It's terrifying to move to a new place, especially if it means being on your own after you've spent so much time with another person, but it's in the middle of those terrifying moments when you recognize your own strength and when you realize that, when all is said and done, you'll make it through. You'll brave the storm. You'll be okay with whatever the hell life hands you.

Granted, not everyone needs to move across the country

to make a change and strike out on their own. Change can come in countless forms. It can be as simple as switching up a hobby (even if you love the ones you have) or researching the possibility of a new job (especially if you hate the one you have) or just picking up and moving across town. The point is that change will bring hope along with it. And hope will bring the promise of a second chance.

L.A. was my second chance.

Here's a little piece of advice I want to share, a piece of wisdom that has served me well as I've faced (and created) change at every level of my life: Look at change as an exciting adventure—even (perhaps *especially*) if you're scared. Rather than looking at it as a frightening prospect that looms on the horizon, look at it as a grand adventure that beckons you from some fresh new place. Adventures, in my mind at least, seem less permanent and scary.

Live your life by holding onto your courage and letting go of your fears. Push yourself beyond your comfort zones. Even when it doesn't feel good. The point is that it will *get* good.

It will get good, eventually.

Too often we just sit around passively, waiting for our condition (or our relationships) to change. Letting life happen to us. Hoping to avoid the worst without taking active steps to create the best.

I'm just going to say it: That's no way to live your life.

As I've been writing this book, I've wanted to make it crystal clear that I'm not encouraging anyone to break up their marriage or make the choice to walk out on their relationship. That's not my role. Not my advice to give.

But you *do* owe it to yourself to be purposeful and pro-active in pushing toward happiness if you're feeling sad. You do need to step up to the plate, be your own change agent, and function as your own catalyst when it's time to make a move.

However you arrive at your happiness is up to you—whether it's through therapy, relationship counseling, breaking up with a partner, severing an unhealthy friendship—whatever your path, try to walk it with confidence.

Search your heart. Carefully research and identify your options. Push past your own paralysis and step into a new way of living—a new way of being. If you don't do it for yourself, it won't get done for you.

I wrote a blog about this very subject a while ago that I want to share:

During the week, we are waiting for the weekend. In the winter, we are waiting for summer. If we have a bad day, we wait for tomorrow to make it better. We wait for life to happen...wait for permission to do things...too scared to look into ourselves, to ask ourselves what it is that we truly want in this moment. Right. Fucking. Now.

But what if we stopped waiting and did something that scares us, today...now, this second?

Even if it doesn't work out, isn't that what life is all about? Taking chances and living in the moment, the risks, excitement, heart racing, madness, the beautiful chaos of the unknown?

So let's go, we are all in this race together. What are you waiting for?

Stop waiting for Friday, for summer, for life. Happiness is achieved when you stop waiting for it and make the most of the moment you are in—right now.

"You cannot swim for new horizons until you have the courage to lose sight of the shore."

—William Faulkner

CHAPTER FOURTEEN

FINDING FORGIVENESS

"True forgiveness is when you can say,
'Thank you for that experience.'"

— Oprah Winfrey

*A*long with true forgiveness comes growth. And along with growth comes the understanding (and acceptance) that every situation you face in life—good or bad, major or minor, memorable or embarrassingly forgettable—can be a learning experience. You can grow from every single one of your life encounters.

This was once a lofty principle that I tried my hardest to attain. Now it's how I try to live my life each day.

This is why I don't regret any moment of my marriage. I don't regret the relationship I had with my ex because without it, I wouldn't be the person I am today.

This is going to sound painfully obvious, but I'm going to say it anyway because to me it has become an essential truth:

What I learned then is what I know now.

Or let me put it another way: *What I learned then is what I AM now.* All that I experienced and everything I encountered became a fundamental part of my fiber. All the ups and downs, all the tangled knots, all the loose ends and frayed edges and confusing moments of self-doubt and paralyzing fear have finally woven themselves together to create a single piece of beautiful fabric: me.

With a lot of hard work, I have finally grown into the person I wanted to become.

When you look at life this way—when you *live* your life this way—forgiveness becomes a part of the natural order of things. Sure, I went through a lot of layers of guilt before reaching this level of forgiveness, but every layer of that guilt—*Did I try hard enough? How could I have allowed the relationship to disintegrate? How could I have let my family and friends down?*—had a purpose.

When you finally realize the person you really need to forgive is yourself, then you are truly able to grow. To move on. To put an end to that never-ending cycle of self-doubt, guilt, and fear so that you can face a brand new day, or perhaps a new life, with positivity and excitement.

Focusing on forgiveness of myself was really the last step in my healing process. I'd been through the pain. I'd been through the guilt. And once I really allowed myself to *learn* from that painful process, to *learn* from all of the mistakes I'd made, the healing began to happen, and I was finally able to give myself permission to move on.

It felt like taking a long, deep breath…a weight lifted.

I'm not going to lie: It's fucking *hard* to forgive yourself, and it might take a long, long time for it to finally happen, but that's okay, too. Finding forgiveness can be a tricky, elusive process;

it can feel like you're playing a game of back-and-forth with yourself. But don't be daunted.

Take baby steps, if you have to. Push yourself toward it. Search for it relentlessly and eventually, after a lot of hard work, you will find it.

Today, right now, as I look back *and* as I look forward, I can comfortably (and confidently) say that finding forgiveness has been one of the best parts of my healing journey.

I don't regret any of the decisions I've made or any of the experiences I've had because I learned from them all. They haven't swallowed me up. If anything, they have *opened* me up. They haven't weakened me at all. If anything, they've strengthened me.

Today, I love (and forgive) the person I used to be, and I also love the person I have become.

It's amazing that in this life I'll have the opportunity to live out a lot of different stories—and instead of looking at that as a negative I can wholeheartedly say it's a good thing.

I'm happy with the woman who is writing to you today.

And *that's* what forgiveness is all about.

"True forgiveness is not an action after the fact; it is an attitude with which you enter each moment."

—David Ridge

CHAPTER FIFTEEN

GETTING TO GRATITUDE

"The struggle ends when gratitude begins."

—Neale Donald Walsch

*W*hen you finally and fully embrace forgiveness, you clear away valuable space for gratitude to step in. You create a more comfortable place in your heart; a more peaceful place where you can stretch out, breathe deeply, and face the world with a positive outlook.

What I'm saying is this: When you get to gratitude, things begin to change. Happiness arrives. The death grip on your heart disappears. Balance returns.

Today, I'm just a lot more *Zen* than I used to be. Gone is the constant search for perfection (although, let's be real, it's always in the back of my mind). No longer do I fill my days with anxiety and endless tasks, trying to people-please everyone, never saying "no" to anyone, and filling my nights with endless angst about what the future will hold for me. I smile more and worry less.

I am honestly the happiest I've ever been in my life.

But as I've said before, unless I'd gone through all that I did with my past relationships, my marriage, my breakup, and eventually my divorce—the ups and downs, the good and the bad, and all the peaks and valleys in between—I wouldn't be at this place of deep contentment. Life isn't always perfect, but you at least owe it to yourself to be real. I wasn't *real* for a very long time, didn't let people see the real Kris because I wasn't perfect all of the time, and I felt that wasn't acceptable.

In order to get to *this* place, I had to travel through those *other* places. Hell no, they weren't always pleasant places to be in. In fact, some of my darkest moments almost pulled me under. But somehow I survived. Somehow I pushed through. With a lot of hard work and purposeful effort, I made it through there to get to here.

It was—and still is—a powerful process, a journey that moved me to an entirely new place that is my life today. I couldn't have arrived here—right now, at this very moment—without first having been there. It was a journey that had to happen, and taking it has finally led me to healing and happiness.

But to get to it, I had to go *through* it—every single step of it. There are no shortcuts. Hell, I would have loved a few shortcuts—a way to make the anger go away quicker, the sadness to heal faster, the confusion and self-doubt to be erased the moment they crept into my head. However, that wouldn't have been true healing, and it wouldn't have led me to the positive place I'm in right now.

Today, I've learned how to put myself first. It might sound selfish, but it's actually one of the most self*less* things I've ever done. Once you realize you need to be your own first priority (even if you're in a relationship), your life begins to change for the better. And if you learn only a few small lessons from this book, let it be these: *Put yourself first. Be honest. Communicate how you actually feel and not what you think people want to hear.*

Love yourself enough to learn from every single mistake you make. Use your breakup as a way to return to your core and to figure out how you truly want to live your life. Not tomorrow. Not next year. But in this very moment.

Figure out how you want to live your life today.

Don't waste precious time on anything that isn't making you happy. It's not up to me to tell you to leave a relationship, but it is up to me to tell you to figure out what the hell is making you unhappy...then fix it.

Today, I no longer walk on eggshells in an attempt to live life like I'm perfect. The perfect person I once pretended to be doesn't exist anymore. I'm not so rigid with my daily life. I hike in the Hollywood Hills, and run on the sand, and surf in the sea. I eat good food with great people, I laugh loud, I hug often, and I smile more times in a day than most people smile in a month.

I've become a better person and a better partner. All of the painful things I've experienced have led to a way more positive person—a stronger one.

Yes, I still believe in marriage, but I no longer believe in the *romanticized* notion of "forever"—it doesn't exist to me anymore because I choose to live in the present moment. Every single day. If you start thinking in "forever," you start to allow life to rush by you because you're so narrowly focused on what is to come instead of simply cherishing *what is.*

Today, I have a new way of looking at the world. It doesn't guarantee that I will always be happy, but it does guarantee that I will always be content and able to handle anything, no matter what situation I am in.

It's a long journey, believe me. But this much I can tell you with certainty, and I hope that these words reach directly into your heart and help guide you on your path as you walk toward happiness again:

You can get there from here.

*"The place to be happy is here.
The time to be happy is now."*

—Robert G. Ingersoll

CLOSING LETTER TO THE READER

So you've made it to the end of what has been, for me, a labor of love–and you've made it here hopefully with a few bits of wisdom, some laughs, and several shakes of your head. The important thing is this: You made it.

I had a lot of reservations about writing this book. I was truly afraid of criticism, of coming off as bitter, of hurting my ex. But when I sat back and gave myself some time to reflect on those thoughts, when I allowed myself the time to really examine my initial reservations, I realized I had a greater goal in mind. I realized this book would be far larger than my own fears—because the message in this book is essentially a happy one, even if there are some hard places you have to make it through to get there.

I wrote this book to help people, to make even one person feel less alone as they are going through a huge shake-up in their lives. It was written with a lot of love and, if I'm being completely honest here, with a fair amount of pain. It was written to show that you can get through a breakup of any kind, no matter how hard the entire process is.

I don't wish a breakup or a divorce on anyone, but if you've decided to take that step, I do hope you'll take to heart some (or all) of the life lessons I've shared within these pages because I speak from experience.

And though our respective experiences are obviously unique, the message I want to share is universal: You can come out the other side of a life-shattering event a stronger, better person if you work through all of the steps properly.

I never wanted to come off as the divorce expert or as the *Conscious Uncoupler* perfect person who gets through a breakup unscathed, mainly because I'm not and I didn't. I made so many missteps throughout the whole process (although I don't regret any of them), and this book is my way of saying that you can make mistakes, you can be really fucking sad, you can drink too much tequila, kiss the wrong people, share a little too much info on social media, you can be angry for no reason at all.

You just can't *stay* in any of those places for too long.

You'll work through all of your shit. You'll laugh and cry (maybe throw things), and eventually you'll look back with a smile. You'll eventually be able to text your ex on their birthday and wish them well (and actually mean it).

You'll hope they meet someone who is good for them and that they have a happy life after you...and because you've worked hard on yourself, you'll be able to heal in a positive way that you never imagined you could. At least this was true for me, and I hope with all of my heart that it is true for you, too.

But you do owe it to yourself to accept and embrace all of the steps that are going to come before you can do any of these things.

Your breakup doesn't have to break *you*. You can take this negative experience and transform it into something positive. Move your heartbreak to an eventually happier place. Call it whatever you want. Here's my suggestion: Call it "breakup positive."

xo,

Kris

"In the end, she became more than what she expected. She became the journey, and like all journeys, she did not end; she just simply changed directions and kept going."

—R.M. Drake

ACKNOWLEDGMENTS

To Ashley, Natalie, Jocelyn, Allison, Vanessa, Cara, and too many others to name. Thank you all for being solid friends and for listening to me when I needed to ramble (which was all the time). For all of the texts you sent to make sure I was okay, to all of the days you let me cry on your shoulders, to every dessert we ate, to every smile you made sure I had on my face. For not judging, for just being there, for letting me be me. I am forever grateful.

To my family, you guys are slightly bananas, but I wouldn't have it any other way. Thanks for letting me spread my wings and for loving me despite all of my ups and downs and backs and forths.

To Mascot Books, for believing in me and letting me write this book. It was such a personal thing to write and an important positive message that you let me share. Thank you so much.

To Kristin, for helping me organize my thoughts (so jumbled at times) so I could better communicate the story I needed to tell.

To Rachel, for your guidance always.

To anyone going through something rough who trusted me enough to buy this book, you aren't alone. We've all been there at some point...I hope I've helped you.

Lastly (but most importantly) to J, a piece of my heart that I didn't even know I was missing until we met. I thought my story was over and then you came along and we've created a whole new chapter in this crazy beautiful life we are living. I love you.